THE HOLY JUMPING-OFF PLACE

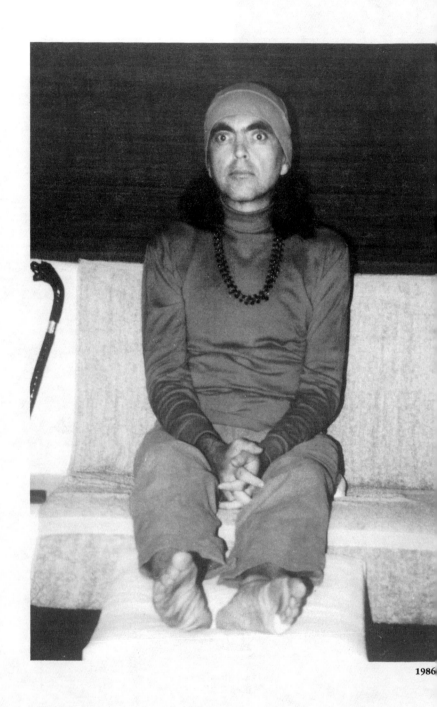

1986

THE HOLY JUMPING-OFF PLACE

An Introduction
to the Way of the Heart
Revealed by
HEART-MASTER DA LOVE-ANANDA

Edited by Ty Koontz

The Dawn Horse Press
San Rafael, California

FOR THE READER

The spiritual practices and functional disciplines discussed in this book, including meditative practices and dietary and sexual disciplines, are appropriate and natural at the progressive stages of practice engaged by members of The Free Daist Communion. Although anyone may find them useful and beneficial, they are not presented as advice or recommendations to the general reader. And nothing in this book is intended as a diagnosis, prescription, or recommended treatment or cure for any specific "problem", whether medical, emotional, psychological, social, or spiritual. One should apply a particular program of diagnosis, treatment, prevention, cure, or general health only with a full understanding of one's state of health and after consultation with a licensed health practitioner or other qualified professional.

Cover photo: "Leaping the Chasm at Stand Rock", 1886, Wisconsin Dells. By permission of the H. H. Bennett Studios, Wisconsin Dells, Wisconsin.

ΕΛΕΥΘΕΡΙΟΣ

First edition—December 1986
Printed in the United States of America
93 92 91 90 89 88 87 86   5 4 3 2 1

International Standard Book Number: paper 0-913922-94-3
Library of Congress Catalog Card Number: 85-72023

Produced by The Free Daist Communion
in cooperation with The Dawn Horse Press

CONTENTS

SECTION ONE

THE LIFE OF HEART-MASTER DA LOVE-ANANDA

The man of understanding is not entranced. He is not elsewhere. He is not having an experience. He is not passionless and inoffensive. He is awake. He is present. He is passionate. His quality is an offense to those who are entranced, elsewhere, contained in the mechanics of experience, asleep, living as various forms of identity, separation and dependence. He is acceptable only to those who understand.

Da Love-Ananda
The Knee of Listening, *p. 269*

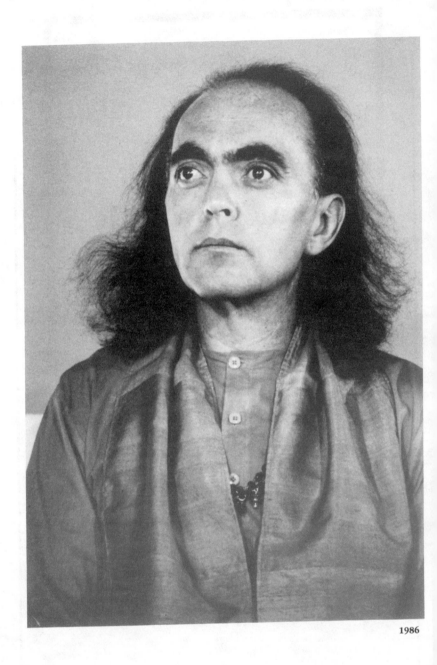

1986

CHAPTER ONE

The Bright Occasion

The Heroic Ordeal of Da Love-Ananda's Realization

Heart-Master Da Love-Ananda was born on November 3, 1939, in Jamaica, Long Island, New York, already Illumined, full of radiant Happiness and the urge to share that Happiness with those around him.

As a baby I remember crawling around inquisitively with an incredible sense of joy, light, and freedom in the middle of my head that was bathed in energies moving freely down from above, up, around and down through my body and my heart. It was an expanding sphere of joy from the heart. And I was a radiant form, a source of energy, bliss and light. I was the Power of Reality, a direct enjoyment and communication. I was the Heart [the Transcendental

---

NOTE TO THE READER: The talks by Heart-Master Da Love-Ananda quoted in this book were given during the sixteen years of Da Love-Ananda's Teaching Work with devotees, from September 1970 through November 1986. Students and beginning practitioners of the Way of the Heart acknowledge Da Love-Ananda as Teacher, or the source of the Wisdom-Teaching, through their study of his Teaching Word and the published records of his Work with devotees during that historic period. But he no longer engages with devotees in face-to-face considerations of the Teaching Argument as he did then. Now he is simply available as the Master of the Heart to those who will respond to his Liberating Heart-Blessing.

Self], who lightens the mind and all things. I was the same as everyone and everything, except it became clear that others were unaware of the thing itself.

Even as a little child I recognized it and knew it, and it was really not a matter of anything else. That awareness, that conscious enjoyment and space centered in the midst of the heart is the "Bright".[1]

Photographs from childhood

In contrast to Da Love-Ananda's complete Freedom and Happiness, the apparent suffering of his family and friends led him, in the third year of his life, to an extraordinary sacrifice. He felt there must be some way for others to know the Joy that was his constant Condition. And, hoping to find the Way, he spontaneously let go of his Happy and Free State, and the "Bright" receded into unconsciousness. He has described the vision of the world that prompted this great sacrifice:

DA LOVE-ANANDA: Franklin Jones [Da Love-Ananda's given name] was born into an ordinary American household. He was not born in a manger, nor was he surrounded by religion and classical art. One would wish to be born in the presence of strong and human and God-Realizing people with kings coming to visit bearing frankincense, myrrh, and gold. But he did not see anything like that. In fact, in the moment he was born, he nearly died. His umbilical cord was wrapped around his neck, and he nearly choked to death. But when he did open his eyes, he was totally conscious of what his surroundings were all about. His entire life is an expression of his prior intuition of Divine Enjoyment. Who knows where it came from? I cannot account for it.

A very difficult vision of existence appeared before him. He saw the stupidity and lovelessness of people's lives, their willingness to tolerate an entire lifetime of frustration, obscenity, fear, and all the things that make men self-possessed. So he took all of that on and lived it, just like you—except he did it consciously, as a service to those who suffer. [2]

During his childhood, the "Bright" at times broke through to guide his spiritual development and reinforce his compassionate impulse to discover a God-Realizing Way of life for modern men and women. These occasions became less and less frequent, however. At last he no longer experienced the "Bright" as a source of Happiness—he had totally assumed the ordinary state of those he wished to help. Now began his great struggle to regain the Realization of inherent Freedom and Joy in order to show the Way for others.

Da Love-Ananda's ordeal of Realization began in 1957 when, at the age of seventeen, he entered Columbia College in New York. For the next thirteen years he drove himself unsparingly, often pushing himself to the point of utter despair in his efforts to overcome the great obstacles that prevent the Liberation of men and women. At Columbia College, he consumed the great works of Western philosophy, but he was disappointed to discover that they held no real capacity to re-Awaken his native Joy.

Then, just as Adepts have traditionally braved the wilderness in search of revelation, he spontaneously embarked on a spiritual quest through the "jungle" of New York City.

Graduating from Columbia College, 1961

He reasoned that if he gave himself uninhibitedly to every possible human experience, the Divine would find some way to make Itself known to him. He threw himself into all the possible experiences New York had to offer. Through the sheer intensity of his seeking, he quickly discovered the dead-ends of the false lure of bodily fulfillment. He pushed himself beyond all ordinary limits until, in 1960, reaching a point of despair with his search, he spontaneously experienced a significant, though short-lived, breakthrough of the Divine Condition that transcends all seeking.

In 1961, he moved to northern California where, during and after graduate work at Stanford University, he explored the vast dimension of psychic phenomena and subtle energies. He discovered Western "occult" literature and Eastern scriptures. Soon he came to feel that to continue his spiritual journey he needed a Teacher, and he had a vision of a small oriental art store in New York City, where he intuited he would find his spiritual Teacher.

California, 1963

Returning to New York in 1964, he discovered the art store, which was run by a spiritual Teacher named Rudi (Albert Rudolph, or Swami Rudrananda), who became Da Love-Ananda's Teacher until 1968. Rudi helped Da Love-Ananda develop basic practical disciplines and spiritual receptivity that prepared his body and mind for his later swift spiritual progress through the mature phases of spiritual practice under Rudi's own Teachers, the Indian Yogis Swami Muktananda Paramahansa and Bhagawan Nityananda. Rudi taught a path of intentional surrender to what he called the "Force", or the Current of spiritual energy felt to descend through the front of the body, purifying and harmonizing body and mind.

At Rudi's request, Da Love-Ananda attended three Christian seminaries, although he no longer considered himself a Christian. While at a Lutheran seminary Da Love-Ananda underwent a dramatic "death event". For three days in the spring of 1967, he was overcome by an increasing anxiety, and he felt certain that he was soon to go mad and die. Nothing that he did could quiet his fears, and finally he consciously allowed the death to happen. This event, which was the death of the ego, permitted the temporary breakthrough of unqualified Consciousness. That breakthrough gave Da Love-Ananda a fundamental insight into the ego and inspired him to develop the spiritual practice of self-enquiry that later led to his final Re-Awakening. And that event also spelled the end of Da Love-Ananda's time with Rudi, since it crystallized his recognition of the limitations of Rudi's yoga of effortful surrender.

In the spring of 1968, Da Love-Ananda traveled to Ganeshpuri, India, to seek out Rudi's Teacher, the Yogi-Adept Swami Muktananda, who at that time was practically unknown in the West. During Da Love-Ananda's three-day stay, he received the initiatory Blessing of three great Yogis: Paramahansa Muktananda, Bhagawan Nityananda (whom Da Love-Ananda contacted in subtle form), and Sri Rang Avadhoot. Under their combined influences, on the last day of his visit, Da Love-Ananda experienced total absorption in Transcendental Consciousness.

This experience catapulted Da Love-Ananda on an intense and rapid journey of spiritual unfolding, which led across three continents and through countless mystical and spiritual experiences as he threw himself into the exploration of traditional esoteric Yoga and mysticism. During a second trip to Ganeshpuri in 1969 Da Love-Ananda received a hand-written letter from Swami Muktananda, acknowledging his right to Teach. But Da Love-Ananda intuited that more was yet to unfold before he would assume the formal role of Heart-Master.

Heart-Master Da Love-Ananda with Swami Muktananda, 1969

After a third trip to Ganeshpuri, Da Love-Ananda was led by a Divine Vision on a holy pilgrimage from India through Europe and ultimately to Los Angeles. His great ordeal had required him not only to understand and go beyond all the ways by which men and women are bound to ordinary existence, but also to experience and transcend the limits of mystical and even spiritual attainment. At last, on September 10, 1970, in a small temple of the Vedanta Society in Hollywood, Da Love-Ananda permanently Re-Awakened to the Realization of the Transcendental Self.

> In an instant, I became profoundly and directly aware of what I am. It was a tacit realization, a direct knowledge in consciousness itself. It was consciousness itself without the addition of a communication from any other source. I simply sat there and knew what I am. I was being what I am. I am Reality, the Self, and Nature and Support of all things and all beings.[3]

Awakening of the Teaching Function

However, Da Love-Ananda's ordeal of Realization was only preparation for the even greater struggle required by his Teaching Work. After the event at the Vedanta Temple, Da Love-Ananda no longer had any personal need to meditate. But when he sat for his customary hours of meditation, he discovered that he was experiencing the content of many people's lives and performing their meditation in his own body-mind:

> DA LOVE-ANANDA: I was aware, visually or otherwise, of great numbers of people, and I would work with them very directly on a subtle level. In some cases, these people would soon contact me and become involved with me in a personal relationship. Others were people I already knew. I would work for them in the subtle way, and then watch for signs and demonstrations in their outward lives of the reality of that manifestation. I tested everything in this manner. [4]

With these signs of the awakening of the Teaching function, Da Love-Ananda began his great ordeal of Teaching Work.

Los Angeles, 1972

At first, Da Love-Ananda Taught only the unadorned Truth of Consciousness that is his Realization. But the ordinary men and women who came to him were unable to practice this pure Teaching. Their personal experiences and difficulties in life consumed nearly all of their energy and attention, so that they had little capacity for the spiritual process. They required more basic lessons in life and beginning spiritual practice before his Blessing could be effectively received.

After several months Da Love-Ananda began to require that those who wished to sit with him in meditation accept a life of functional, practical, and relational disciplines that would allow them to live a more balanced, healthy, and ordinary life and that would free energy and attention for the spiritual process. Yet Da Love-Ananda soon saw that these disciplines alone were not sufficient to transform the individuals who came to him and to prepare them for mature spiritual practice. They needed an entire culture of human development and spritual preparation—and he would have to create it!

Heart-Master Da Love-Ananda with students, 1974

Just as he had thrown himself without reservation into his own ordeal of Realization, he now gave himself utterly to the struggle of his devotees. For over sixteen years he engaged students and practitioners in a passionate ordeal for their sakes, arguing his great Wisdom-Teaching to them face to face, living through their own spiritual trials with them, and magnifying the inherent Happiness of Realization in the midst of their lives. Showing a diligence and persistence they were not yet capable of, he brought to light all the obstructions in their lives that prevented their spiritual growth. He examined with them their relationships to each other and to him, helping them feel all the hiding, defensiveness, and thoughtless aggression that kept them from living as Love. And he helped them understand and transcend their emotional neuroses in the areas of work, marriage, health, diet, social relations, and so on. Giving himself tirelessly on their behalf, he brought them through countless lessons, revealing in every instance and to each one the understanding that penetrates all apparently binding conditions.

When Da Love-Ananda first began to Teach, he was still known by his given name, "Franklin Albert Jones". In 1973, during a trip to India to purify his relationship to the Teachers who had served his own spiritual practice, he spontaneously assumed the name "Bubba Free John". "Free John" is a rendering of "Franklin Jones", which literally means "a free man through whom God is Gracious". And "Bubba", his childhood nickname, which means "brother", indicated his willingness to live with students and practitioners as a spiritual Friend until they could recognize him in Truth and relate to him formally as Heart-Master. Then, in 1979, after a period of weaning devotees from dependence on his physical Company and instructing them in the formal spiritual relationship to him, he assumed the sacred name "Da", meaning "Giver" or "the one who Gives or Transmits the Divine Influence and Awakening to living beings".

The Name "Da" is particularly appropriate for Da Love-Ananda, since he has Blessed devotees and all humanity with countless gifts. During his Teaching Work, he not only generated an immense body of written and spoken instruction, he also Blessed and Empowered three meditation Sanctuaries (The Mountain of Attention in northern California, Tumomama in Hawaii, and Translation Island in Fiji) each containing many holy sites where his Transmission of Blessing and Awakening Power is concentrated and magnified to quicken the spiritual process in his devotees. He has also inspired the creation of a worldwide sacred institution and instructed and initiated an entire community of devotees in the Way of the Heart. These human Agencies are now potent vehicles of his Blessing.

1981

His Grand Victory and Blessing Work

Despite Da Love-Ananda's many gifts to his devotees, his extraordinary Teaching Work had only a limited effect. Devotees certainly became happier, more functional, and more responsible, and a profound and enduring love-relationship formed between the Heart-Master and his devotees. But devotees persisted in the beginning stages of spiritual life, refusing the ultimate Gift of Liberation and the Realization of the Divine Condition.

The stubborn refusal of the ego to bow to Truth is almost universally underestimated, even though the sacred traditions are filled with examples of rejection of the Heart-Master's gift of Blessing and even betrayal of the Heart-Master himself.

Only the Heart-Master feels the full burden of the struggle that is the spiritual process, for the devotee's Way is eased by the great sacrifice consciously and freely undertaken by the Adept. Yet even with Da Love-Ananda's great help, to live the Way of the Heart requires everything of a man or woman. Inevitably, the ancient drama of rejection unfolds in each person's case as the ego-bound individual, reaching the limit of his ability to practice real spiritual life, hardens his heart to the Adept's call. This is the most difficult test for every devotee, and to pass beyond it requires a conversion to love that is uncommon in human history. Meanwhile, the Heart-Master, who is utterly vulnerable, suffers the destructive self-possession of his devotees as a deep and never-healing wound.

The unanimous refusal of his devotees to receive his Gift of Realization brought Da Love-Ananda to the crisis that culminated in an event that he has said is more significant for his Work than his Realization at the Vedanta Temple. He came to feel that his Work was doomed to fail because humanity was not ready to accept the supreme Gift of Liberation. After more than sixteen years of the most thorough and inspired Teaching Work, Da Love-Ananda despaired of his sole purpose in life—to fully Awaken a significant number of men and women. And at Translation Island, the Hermitage Sanctuary in Fiji, early on the morning of January 11, 1986, reaching the moment of utmost despair, Heart-Master Da Love-Ananda gave up his Teaching Work and abandoned the body.

As the process of death progressed and the signs of life began to depart his body, his personal physicians and a few of his closest devotees rushed to his residence. Before long, the flickering signs of life began to stabilize and then to grow stronger, and before the death process became irreversible, Da Love-Ananda re-entered the body once more. As he said later, he was moved to live again because of the deepest Love for his devotees and all beings, even though he felt certain that no one was yet prepared to receive what he had to offer. Although he restored himself to life, his relinquishment of his Teaching Work in the moment of death was (as he would make clear in the following months) final.

Paradoxically, only in the relinquishment of his Teaching Work was the means for its fulfillment brought into being. Drawn to life by his Love for devotees, Da Love-Ananda assumed the human condition without reservation, with nothing to shield himself from sorrow and death. In this Great Event Heart-Master Da Love-Ananda incarnated his Divine Realization and Love more fully than ever before, and this transformation had profound effects upon his Work with devotees. He has called this event his "Grand Victory", for, as devotees came to see in the months that followed, in his effortless, complete, Loving embrace of humanity, Heart-Master Da Love-Ananda's Divine Agency was magnified beyond compare.

Shortly after this turning point, he adopted the name "Love-Ananda", meaning "the Divine Love-Bliss"—the outstanding characteristic of his Realization and his Gift to devotees.

Now, finished with his efforts to Teach, Da Love-Ananda Shines as the Heart, Transmitting his Heart-Blessing freely to all, Awakening men and women throughout the world to the intuition of always present Happiness, or Love-Bliss. Through the spiritual initiation and Transmission abundant in Da Love-Ananda's spiritual Company, devotees are given the Revelation of the Divine Person, the Self of all, the One Consciousness by Whose Power and Grace even ordinary men and women may be forever Liberated from bondage to this world of fleeting pleasures and certain pain.

Translation Island, 1986

SECTION TWO

THE TEACHING ARGUMENT

*A*ll *I have asked is that you*
understand.
It is a simplicity, signalled
in many ways.
Do not imagine it is more or less
than my plain word,
the time you heard me and understood.

Da Love-Ananda
The Knee of Listening, *p. 206*

1978

CHAPTER TWO

It Is a Simplicity

two conversations with
Heart-Master Da Love-Ananda

Much of Da Love-Ananda's published literature is the record of his responses to the actual questions of the men and women who came to him. He did not sit in isolation, generating abstract philosophy and idealistic instructions, but he Worked directly with men and women in the midst of their daily lives. Many of the major Arguments of his Wisdom-Teaching were developed in conversation with students and practitioners, whose real needs drew the instruction from him. The following two conversations give only a taste of the vitality, humor, and passion of the Heart-Master's great Teaching Work.

Remember the Mystery in Which You Live

The following conversation between Da Love-Ananda and a young boy named Ian took place on October 28, 1978, at The Mountain of Attention Sanctuary, the principal site of pilgrimage and retreat for devotees. In an open-air pavilion Da Love-Ananda, dressed in white, sat before a large gathering. As devotees came to a microphone in the center of the room and spoke directly to the Heart-Master, he responded to their questions about spiritual practice.

IAN: Master, I have a personal discipline not to be righteous. But I'm still righteous a lot, and I can't really find a way to stop it.

DA LOVE-ANANDA: What do you mean "righteous"?

IAN: Well, I try to be smart, you know. I do things like telling somebody something, just walking by somebody and saying something to him, not really meaning it, just being rude.

DA LOVE-ANANDA: Are you angry about something?

IAN: I'm angry when I say it.

DA LOVE-ANANDA: What are you angry about?

IAN: Well, I'm just inside myself.

DA LOVE-ANANDA: Why do you think you are angry? Do you feel angry a lot?

IAN: Not too much, but sometimes I feel real angry.

DA LOVE-ANANDA: Is being righteous a way of being angry?

IAN: Yes.

DA LOVE-ANANDA: So?

IAN: Do you have a way that you can tell me that I can stop being righteous? [Everyone in the room laughs, enjoying the simple honesty of the young boy.]

DA LOVE-ANANDA: Yes. If you love. If you will love people and persist in that feeling, allow yourself to love people all the time, then you will not be righteous in the way that you are talking about. It is fine every now and then to tell somebody where he (or she) is at. [Laughter.] You have to be able to know the difference between behavior in people that is all right and behavior that is not all right, that is negative. But if you love them, then you will know the difference between the things they do that are good and the things that are not. And you will be able to talk to them about the things that are not good without being righteous, without being angry, you see. You will be able to be Happy with them because you will know at that moment that you also love them. Whereas when you are being righteous, you are not aware of the fact that you love them. You forget about that for a minute.

You have to learn about this loving feeling. Whenever we do not love, whenever we do not feel in this world, we start getting angry. And after we have been angry for a long time, we start getting afraid. We start to feel bad. So we have to learn how to be able to love all the time, how to feel all the time. We have to be able to feel the world. A lady who was just talking to me said she gets up in the morning unhappy about the fact that the world exists. Well, the mood that she was in at that moment is not the mood of a practitioner. A practitioner wakes up and, even though things may not be going too well, he feels God. He knows God is all over this world, all inside the world, you see, inside everyone and outside everyone. He feels that the world is about God, that the world is about Love. But people who are not being Happy do not know that the world is about God. They do not know that the world is about Love. That is why they do not love very much. That is why they are always talking about themselves and about negative things.

So, if you are angry and righteous, it is just that you have forgotten for a moment that the world is about God, and that the world is about Love, and that you are about Love. And there is nothing you can do about being righteous if you forget to love, if you forget that the world is about God. You cannot stop being righteous by trying not to be righteous. You will stop being righteous when you forget about being righteous, which means you have to remember to love. *What to Remember to Be Happy*—I have written a book on the subject.

You are all the time remembering what you have to remember to be angry and righteous. Instead, you have to remember what you have to remember in order to be Happy, and that means you have to remember God. You have to remember the Mystery in which you live. You have to remember to love, and you have to love, and you have to practice loving people. Do not wait for it to just happen. You have to practice loving people. And you have to communicate love to them. You have to say you love them. You have to do things for them that are full of the feeling of love for them. You see? So, find out what you have to remember to be Happy and do that. If you do that, then you will forget to be angry and righteous.

And sometimes you may have something to say to somebody about something that he (or she) is doing that is not very good, but it will not be the same as righteousness. You will tell this to him because you love him. And when you tell him, you will even sound like you love him. There are even bad people here and there. You probably have not met any really bad people lately, not any really bad ones. But even the really bad ones are alive in the same world. They are with God just like you. They have some things to learn, but you cannot teach them without loving them. You cannot teach anybody anything without being Happy with them. And you cannot be Happy with anybody else unless you are Happy. You cannot always wait for others to do something to make you Happy, you see. You have to be Happy, and then you make other people Happy, too.

Dancing Completely Madly and Completely Happily

During a gathering with devotees in early October 1976, Da Love-Ananda turned to a devotee named Paris and quietly suggested to him that he "get up and dance completely madly and completely Happily." Paris could not do it—nor, as Da Love-Ananda went around the room with his request, could anyone else. After all had failed the test, he said:

> *The whole matter of Enlightenment is to Realize complete Happiness as the body, in every moment, to look and feel and be and act completely Happy as the body. I suggest to you all that you will not be Enlightened until you can get up and dance. I would not go to bed tonight if I had not done this, if I were any of you!*

Paris was scheduled to give a talk on meditation to the assembled membership in Western Face Cathedral, one of the meditation halls at The Mountain of Attention Sanctuary. Within moments after he began, the Heart-Master interrupted him to challenge him once again to get up and dance madly and ecstatically before the entire assemblage.

DA LOVE-ANANDA: Let me tell you this right now, Paris, there is no way that you are going to get out of this room this afternoon without dancing for us completely madly. [Laughing and clapping.] I will consider that to be a sufficient statement from you on the subject of meditation. Otherwise, you are going to have to give a very, very long presentation. [Laughter.] Apart from your dancing, nobody here is going to know what dancing is, you see. Apart from your meditation, no one is going to know what it is. So what we require is a demonstration from you. [Laughter and clapping.] Completely madly and completely Happily. Get Up!!! [Paris makes a move to get up, but he cannot do it.] Get him up, somebody. You—you dance with him. [Now other devotees, as self-conscious as Paris, laughingly refuse to dance. Da Love-Ananda is laughing uproariously.] Stand up! Dance!!! <u>Dance</u>!!! [Although all are laughing with delight and even some embarrassment, no one is dancing. The Heart-Master waits until the rumpus has subsided a bit, and then he makes his point.]

Well, you see what it comes down to. It is not whether or not you have understood me. It is whether you will do it or not. I think after all that has been said and done in all these years, it really is not necessary for me to go on saying and doing a lot of unique things, trying to make the point to you all. I think that point is made. You know very well what it is all about. And at least you have plenty of tape recordings to renew your consideration! But I need no longer communicate it. That essentially has been done. Now it comes down to whether or not you will do it.

You know precisely what it would be to look and feel and be <u>completely</u> Happy in this moment. It is inherent. It is the condition of your birth, this Happiness. You cannot know about it in all kinds of technical ways or justify it. You can only be it. You can only dance or not. Nothing will convince you of it and nothing makes it possible and nothing will make it easy.

You all are waiting for some sort of significant communication or miracle that will allow you to dance, to love, to be completely Happy in all of your appearances in this moment. You are waiting for a sign from somewhere because you are bound in your subjectivity to your separateness, your isolation. You separate from all other forces the energy you represent singly, and you do not dance. That is all there is to it.

There is no such thing as gradual dancing. [Laughter.] There is no way to learn how to dance, to be Happy, to be Radiant. You know what it is to be completely Happy in this moment. It is not that you know about it in your head. Sitting here, you know what it would be to look and feel and be completely Happy. Already you know this, you see. You are simply not doing it. And we can get together and pretend that somehow, by my talking to you or doing this and that, you will become convinced to do it. But I will not convince you, and it will always be as difficult as it appears to you in this moment.

DEVOTEE: I will dance for you, Master.

DA LOVE-ANANDA: Let's see it. [Laughter and clapping.] Completely madly and completely Happily. No music and no program, no learned steps, completely madly and completely Happily. Completely! Completely!!!

[Waiting once again for the hilarity to pass, the Heart-Master continues.] That was a modest attempt. But, you see, being asked to look and feel and be completely Happy or to dance completely madly, completely Happily, is like Rudi's saying to me several years ago. "Surrender! Surrender completely!" To dance and look in certain ways and so forth is to do what I have asked, but, you see, you cannot dance any more than you can surrender. And if you did dance, as someone just attempted to do, your dancing would be filled with all of the learned dancing and self-consciousness that are inherently your self-presentation.

Therefore, the method of dancing does not work. [Laughter.] It is just a way of creating a lesson in this moment so that you will see how profoundly you are bound to your self-consciousness. And when, in your Enlightenment, you are relieved of this point of view, you will act silly and do bizarre things in the company of others. Whatever you do will be dancing, whatever you do will be Happiness and loving, whatever it is, however it appears.

Every moment, every kind of action, and every process is a kind of dancing in your Enlightenment. You do not have to dance especially. Actually, as soon as you try the method of dancing, you will become convinced of your dilemma again, your separation. So it is a rather easeful matter, not a matter of doing all the things that might embarrass you, or doing all the things that are difficult for you to do.

As time went on with Rudi I began to feel that I could never surrender until I could do all the things that I absolutely did not want to do. I did incredible things to myself that I did not want to do, in order to surrender everything, and it absolutely does not work. After a while you become so depressed. [Laughter.] You are standing in front of everyone flinging your body around like a mad person, and you are not Happy, not dancing wildly, not being Happy.

DEVOTEE: Master, will you dance?

DA LOVE-ANANDA: Absolutely not! [Laughter.]

DEVOTEE: You are dancing!

DA LOVE-ANANDA: Exactly! [Laughter.] Whatever I may appear to be doing, I am completely Happy in this moment. To get up and do some exaggerated thing for your benefit would not seem to me to be very Happy, as it likewise does not seem to you to be. Dancing is not the point. It is just a way of considering your ordinary position, the refusal to dance when you are asked to, the inability to be completely free of self-consciousness when you are asked to present yourself.

What it comes down to is that there is no method of

dancing. What appears as ordinary life is absurd, ridiculous, intolerable. There is nothing to do but to throw it all away, to let everything go. But that is not a method, you see. It is not like dancing in the company of others completely madly and completely Happily in some entertaining fashion.

Happiness is not a matter of doing something that is Radiant and Happy. It is a matter of this consideration, the realization and the tacit knowledge that whatever is occurring in this moment is dance, is Happiness, is Radiance. Life is a matter of recognition, then, not action or strategy. You cannot surrender—you must be surrendered. You cannot sacrifice, you must be sacrifice. Therefore, I advise you to give up all remedies altogether in this consideration. In your Enlightenment, you see, you are Radiant and you are Happy and you are love and you are dancing, and in the natural course, you will find all the new ways whereby life is dancing.

That ought to be enough for today.

CHAPTER THREE

What Are You Always Doing?

What Do We All Believe?

What is mankind's most widespread, most deep-rooted belief? What article of faith is maintained so adamantly and professed so universally, that, with the exception of a handful of people throughout history, it has been adopted by every member of every cultural and social group on the face of this planet?

This common belief, uniquely affirmed by every person, is that each one of us is an "I", an individual self completely separate from all other beings and things. This is so obviously true for us that we hardly give it a passing thought. It is the organizing principle of all our experience, the "plain truth" of our existence. Our very language is founded on this conviction of selfhood. We even capitalize the "I" reference. As Da Love-Ananda once expressed it, "Ordinary speech and written language are centered on the ego-'I', as a tent is raised on a centerpole."[1]

What is perhaps most remarkable about this belief, which hardly anyone questions, is that when we are Enlightened, we can see that it simply is not true! Da Love-Ananda is one of those rare few who have gone beyond the confining belief that the human being is identical to a limited and mortal body-mind. His testimony, like that of other Adepts or God-Realized Beings before him, is that anyone can be free of "the cramp of the self", or the ego-"I", in Reality. No such "I" exists, he proclaims, not even in your own case!

To Da Love-Ananda, the ordinary life is something like a dream:

> DA LOVE-ANANDA: You can remember meeting people in your dreams, can you not? You now know that then you were only dreaming. Everything you saw or experienced was arising in your own consciousness. You presented yourself to yourself in the form of somebody else. You had adventures with all kinds of people and in all kinds of places, but the places, the people, everything you experienced, could have been nothing other than modifications of your own psyche. That is exactly the case in this moment, except that this is not a dream in the sense that you are off sleeping someplace. Your relationship to this moment, however, is precisely the same as your relationship to the moment of the dream. All of this is arising as the modification of your own existence.
>
> You are a dreamer who is not aware that he or she is dreaming. I, however, am a dreamer who is Awake, and who sees you as himself, a modification of his own being, or the very Being with Whom he is perfectly Identified. Thus, I do not spend my life trying to escape this world. The attempt to escape or avoid life is a fretful effort of the ego, the one who does not understand but only reacts fearfully to his or her condition. Therefore, I spend my time talking to and living among people in the dream in such a fashion that I am always agitating them to Awaken, as I have, to understand the Condition of this world. That is what people naturally and spontaneously do when they wake up: They understand. [2]

In his efforts to help others understand, Da Love-Ananda spent more than sixteen years in Teaching people. During that time he generated thousands of talks and essays, many of which are published in the over thirty volumes of literature. The first step in the process of understanding is to study his Teaching Argument and to begin to apply it to your life. Da Love-Ananda calls this initial practice "listening" or "pondering and preparation". To "listen" is a profound practice of granting full attention to the arguments, questions, and lessons of the Wisdom-Teaching.

Beyond the Search for the Great Secret

What is the secret that, if we could only find it out, would allow us to feel happy, completely Happy, under any circumstance? Everyone longs for such secret knowledge, and religious traditions all over the world point to just such a hidden treasure. How does one find the enigmatic secret that Jesus praised as "the peace that passeth all understanding"? What is the mysterious Realization that Gautama Buddha conveyed in his "Four Noble Truths" concerning the Way beyond suffering? What did Krishna Realize and proclaim as the Bliss of the Self?

Such questions reflect a wonder and a desire to understand our purpose here that is more or less universal among human beings. Throughout human history men and women have attempted to discover why we are here and where we are going. This great quest has also led many men and women to seek out Heart-Master Da Love-Ananda. But the motive of seeking is self-centered, thus reinforcing our false identification with the "I" who is suffering.

The search itself was one of the first things Da Love-Ananda found necessary to address in the men and women who came to him.

From the beginning, Da Love-Ananda has made no concessions to "the seeker". Instead, he has pointed out over and over again that our search for the ultimate answer may be necessary initially, but it soon becomes a futile and deluding undertaking. It distracts us from the real discovery that we need to make, the very discovery that makes spiritual life possible. And that discovery is not about a solution or an achievement or a technique. It is about ourselves. It is radical, or summary, or irreducible, insight into the search itself and its motivations.

If we pause for a moment from the search to examine the act of seeking, we will inevitably come to see that the search itself is an admission of present unhappiness. If I am Happy, why seek? If I have already found the Truth that brings unreasonable and unlimited Joy, why look for It?

Indeed, the grand spiritual adventure, the mighty quest for Truth, tends to prevent us from seeing and understanding our actual, present unhappiness. Examine your daily life. You can see that you are involved in a search in every moment, not just the great, meaningful moments. Our every action is driven by the desire for Happiness, from the momentary scratch of an itch to the endeavor of a lifetime. We are rarely simply Happy. Our moments of Happiness are occasional and brief.

The search, rather than bringing us Happiness, binds us to rituals of unhappiness. To seek is to postpone Happiness, to place it in the future at the end of our journey. But the Truth we seek, as Da Love-Ananda points out, must be just as True of the present moment as it is of any future moment.

> Whatever is the Truth, it must be True at this moment. It must be always already True, both in and prior to every moment of space-time. Therefore, the Realization of Truth is not attained in the search for Truth, since seeking must necessarily bypass the Truth in this moment in order to pursue it as an eventual Goal of action in time and space.[3]

What Are You Always Doing?

Suppose you and a friend each take up an end of a twenty-foot rope, stretching it taut between you. Have your friend give the rope a good shake, and a ripple will roll through the rope toward you. Eventually the ripple will reach you, moving your hand and arm in a kind of long-distance handshake with your friend. However, if you both shake the rope at once and with approximately the same force, the two ripples will roll to meet each other and, exchanging greetings at the center, will more or less cancel each other out.

Now imagine a tub full of water with a device in the center that creates ripples. Using the canceling effect of counter-ripples, consider trying to create enough counter-ripples to make the water smooth. You can easily see that the task is impossible. You simply cannot make enough counter-ripples quickly enough to cancel every ripple. Furthermore, the act of forming counter-ripples produces new ripples that must themselves be countered. The only way to restore the water to calmness is to forget counter-measures entirely and simply stop the action that is generating the ripples in the first place.

This situation, explains Da Love-Ananda, resembles our common dilemma:

> DA LOVE-ANANDA: You can be busy trying to smooth out the ripples all over the body-mind, but you never straighten them out. Smooth one out, and another one appears, and then you discover the first one is there again!
>
> Just so, you can work on the mind and the emotions and the body and your relationships, you can busy yourself trying to straighten out your life, but life never gets straightened out. You can do self-improvement work and make your life a little better, but you cannot become Enlightened, you cannot become Happy, through these efforts. You must directly and presently observe, understand, and transcend the source of un-Happiness. [4]

The radical message of Da Love-Ananda's Teaching Argument is that the source of dilemma and unhappiness in our lives, like the device creating ripples in the center of the tub, is our own doing. It is our constant activity—not something that happens to us, not something inherent in the scheme of things, but something we are always doing, unceasingly, automatically, unconsciously. And this activity ripples through every event of our lives.

It may seem hard to believe, and it is certainly paradoxical, but in every moment we are the source of our own unhappiness. In fact, so consistent is our creation of unhappiness that most of the time we are hardly even aware of it.

Consider this remark by Da Love-Ananda: "If any one Will Feel and Examine his or her state In any moment, Whether Under the worst Or the best Or the most ordinary of circumstances, he or she Will Surely Discover That There Is Always A Characteristic Feeling Of Stress, or Dis-ease, or A Motivating Sense Of Dilemma."[5]

Consider your feeling right now. You are probably in a physically comfortable position as you read this. But if you feel more thoroughly into your bodily state, you will undoubtedly notice small aches or itches, tight muscles, hunger or thirst, tiredness or tension, places where your clothing pinches a little or constricts your movement, or any number of other minor discomforts. But even aside from all of that you can imagine feeling really good—beyond merely being free of minor disturbances—feeling, as Da Love-Ananda often expresses it, "pleasure in all your cells".

And the same consideration no doubt applies to your emotional state. You probably feel relatively calm and happy. But remember how good you felt when you fell in love? And beyond that, think what it would be like to be completely happy, completely Happy! You could be feeling absolutely radiant—in this moment. Over against that, you can easily see that your present emotional state is less than full Happiness.

And what about your mental state? As anyone who has ever meditated knows, let your mind run free for only a few minutes and you will inevitably witness a stream of countless small worries, things that need to be done, unresolved situations from the past, and so on.

"Wait," you say. "Yes, I can imagine feeling better, being happier, and being free of disturbing thoughts, but life is just like that." And that is the point. We have come to accept a profoundly limited condition as being somehow necessary. We are habituated to suffering. And the suffering we have just been considering is only the most superficial. If you can allow yourself to drop below the surface of things, you will notice a profound anxiety, a feeling of being trapped in a mortal and threatened existence. This root fear colors every moment of our lives, producing stress at all levels of our being. That fear is the inevitable accompaniment of our assumption that each of us is a defined and limited "I", completely separate from all other beings and things. That assumption is the root action that is our unhappiness.

Our suffering is single, but so true of us it is everywhere and universally displayed. We are each one possessed of a lie, believed from our experience. Our experience, however factual, is not Truth. The lie is not merely subjective, but seems to be proven even in the structures of this solid world, the dream in which we are all involved. Until we awaken, the worlds of all arising, within and without, oblige us by this lie and stand forth as the very theatre of this lie.

The lie is single, irreducibly true of us in the dream. It is the belief each of us has that "I" is my Condition, that the Truth of me is within, in the form of an inner or subjective self, existing prior to and presently or even eternally independent of all other selves, objects, and conditions, and not in any sense arising as a dependent function of relations, like a shape or a thing, but separate, deep, shapeless but unique, and inside, like a bird in a cage. [6]

1972

CHAPTER FOUR

The Open Hand

Narcissus, the Hidden Logic of "I"

Da Love-Ananda calls the root of our suffering "Narcissus". The myth of Narcissus is an archetype of the action that is our suffering. According to Greek mythology, Narcissus was a handsome young man who one day saw his reflection in a woodland pond. Without recognizing his own face, Narcissus fell in love with the reflected image of himself, which he took to be another. From that moment, he sat by the pond staring at his reflected image, utterly self-absorbed. There he lingered until he died, with no attention for anything but his own reflection. The tragedy of the story, of course, is that the image was only an illusion—there was no "other" to give or receive love in his self-enclosed world.

When, during his own spiritual ordeal, Da Love-Ananda uncovered the hidden logic of Narcissus at work in himself, he recognized in Narcissus the mechanism that is suffering itself. And he was struck by the pervasive character of this mechanism.

The more I contemplated [Narcissus] the more profoundly I understood him. I witnessed in awe the primitive control that this self-concept and logic performed in all of my behavior and experience. I began

41

to see that same logic operative in all other men and
every living thing, even the very life of the cells and
the energies that surround every living entity or
process. It was the logic or process of separation
itself, of enclosure and immunity. It manifested as
fear and identity, memory and experience. It informed every function of being, every event. It created every mystery. It was the structure of every
imbecile link in the history of our suffering. [1]

Clearly, Da Love-Ananda's insight into Narcissus goes far
beyond any conventional approach to this myth. For Da Love-
Ananda, Narcissus is not a symbol of mere selfishness, or an
archetype of vanity or pride or even necessarily negative
human qualities. Narcissus is equally the foundation logic of
our so-called "good" behavior. Narcissus is the core of our
entire life of suffering, our ordinary destiny.

No matter what our character, at the foundation of our
identity is the sense of separation. Whoever "I" am, "I" am
completely separate from "you", or any of the "other" people
and things "I" see. We define ourselves by an act of separation—the conscious differentiation between "self" and all
"others". This is one of the very first behaviors we learn as
babies. And from then on, our lives are dedicated to the
survival and happiness of that separate one. This sense of
separation and self-obsession is Narcissus.

But, just as Narcissus' lover was only an illusion created
by his own reflection, the ego-"I" is only a presumption,
based on the activity of separation itself. In the following
passage, Da Love-Ananda cuts to the core of Narcissus, simply
and clearly outlining the mechanism of our sense of
separation.

DA LOVE-ANANDA: You must have listened to music
through a pair of stereo speakers or headphones. The
sound appears to arise from some point in the middle of your head. The psycho-physical organism as a
whole operates in very much the same way. The
functional mechanisms of perception, such as the

ears, seem to "target" phenomena. When we are weak, when we have suffered through not living these phenomena from the point of view of Truth, we become obsessed with this point of awareness, the target itself. We begin to <u>identify</u> with it. Perception or experience creates the self, the ego, and we begin chronically to live in terms of this target as if it were the source and center of life.

No matter what phenomena arise, you habitually manipulate them in such a way that this target becomes the focus and apparent source or origin of your attention. This target becomes the chronic implication of all experience.

This avoidance of relationship, this contraction, is what is always going on. And, we buy it! We continually buy it. I often make a fist out of my hand to indicate this activity to you, because it shows very clearly what happens when there is this contraction. If you curl your hand in upon itself, a sensation is created at the center of the hand that concentrates attention. This sensation in the hand is differentiated from every possible thing that is outside it. It becomes the center of concentration. The same process, generated in the psycho-physical life as a whole, becomes the point of view toward all of this, whereas it is only a functional reflection of various forces. At every level of consciousness, the entire psycho-physical mechanism is devoted to this activity, this curling in upon itself. This is Narcissus.

Every moment of life is devoted to the creation of this "point". And this contraction ultimately becomes terminal. It becomes psycho-physical death, because it is endlessly intensified, to the point of absolute contraction, so there is no longer any flow of force. If I hold my hand clenched tightly in a fist, increasing the tension, so that no blood will flow, it will eventually wither. So men are dying of this one activity. [2]

Da Love-Ananda's analogy of the fist illustrates the futility of all seeking and all attempts to become Happy, to improve Narcissus or change his situation in order to achieve Happiness. All such attempts are like trying to make a fist feel better. If you hold your hand in a fist so long that it becomes painful, there is nothing you can do to the fist that will really help. You can try to soak it in water to relieve the pain, or put it on ice, or lay it on soft pillows, or cover it with all kinds of ointments. You can endow it with a trust fund and make it the wealthiest fist in the world. You can dress it in fine cloth, or use it for charitable causes, or put it on retreat in a silent cave, or wedge incense between its fingers and use it in rituals of worship. But if you continue to make the fist, you will continue to suffer.

The "I" that is you, Narcissus, the one who is the avoidance of relationship, never gets better. And the life of Narcissus is necessarily a life of suffering. Like Narcissus, you have devoted all your attention to a lost cause—your "self"! Without ever really considering it, you have become committed to a painful mode of existence. If you could only break free of your spell of self-enchantment, you would discover that your suffering is just as unnecessary as the mythical plight of Narcissus at his solitary pond.

Breaking the Spell

In his more than sixteen years of dialog with those who came to him, Da Love-Ananda created an entire Way of life and a culture of spiritual practice in his efforts to awaken people from their trance of self-enchantment. The beginning, or "listening" and "pondering", stage of the Way of the Heart is simply to study his Wisdom-Teaching and to consider his Argument in the actual circumstances of your own life. His Teaching Argument is supremely practical. It is meant to be applied directly to your daily existence, so that you might discover the truth of it for yourself. Da Love-Ananda has repeatedly urged people to go beyond the tendency to settle for mere belief or intellectual understanding of his communication and to actually test his Argument in life.

DA LOVE-ANANDA: You must not accept the Teaching as absolute doctrines that you are supposed to believe. That is not it at all. The Teaching is not presented to you as a series of propositions. It is presented to you as a consideration, something for you to enter into and observe yourself over against. Discover whether it is true. Discover its use. Make use of it, in other words, and do not merely believe it. The more you learn through such consideration, the more you become involved in real practice.[3]

This practice of listening or pondering provides the foundation for the entire Way. If pursued with real intention, this humble and ordinary practice yields a great revelation. Simply apply the Argument about Narcissus, the self-contraction, to your own experience. Test this Argument in your life until you actually see Narcissus. This will not be an intellectual perception, but you will feel the contraction as your present action. Narcissus is a disease of feeling that pervades every moment of our lives, the good as well as the bad.

This might sound like a dreadful thing to discover about yourself. If not for the intuition of prior Happiness, it really would be dreadful. The process leading to this discovery can be something of an ordeal, because Narcissus mightily resists exposure, even to himself. But the moment of penetrating insight, the moment when you are thoroughly convicted of being Narcissus, turns out to be surprisingly good news! Then you do not recognize Narcissus alone. Once Narcissus is exposed to view, what your Narcissistic activity was hiding—your true Condition—also comes to light.

The liberating lesson of real self-observation is that the life of Narcissus, the self-contracted existence that is always turning back upon itself, is not necessary—it is unnatural, an imposition on your true Condition. In the course of Da Love-Ananda's own spiritual unfolding this became clear to him in a moment when, at the age of twenty-five, he contemplated his own hand:

All Of My Years Of Practice Were Founded On The

Same Basic Insight, and Those Years Were Punctuated
By Sudden Great Leaps Of Understanding. One Such
Moment Of Awakening and Insight Occurred Quite
Gently In 1965, In A Moment In Which I Was Mind-
lessly Regarding My Right Hand, Observing The Dif-
ference Between The Natural or Open and Func-
tionally Relational Attitude Of The Hand and The
Unnatural or Contracted and Functionally Dissoci-
ated Attitude Of The Clenched Fist. The Natural Sign
Of the human body Is Relatedness, Not Separation
and Independence! When This Sign Convicted The
Heart, The subjective Commitment To self-Contrac-
tion Was Spontaneously Released. In That Moment
There Was A Quiet Revolution In This Body-Mind. I
Knew The Always Already State.[4]

When it becomes absolutely clear—not merely mentally
but feelingly, in your whole being—that you are doing unhappiness, you naturally, even instantly, drop it. And in that
moment the Happiness that is your native Condition breaks
through. It is as if, in the midst of applying one more ointment
to your painfully clenched fist, you realize all you need to do
is open your hand. What a relief! It is the most natural and
easy thing to do. What freedom! You can throw away your
medicine chest. Everything you thought you needed to make
your fist feel better is unnecessary. Suddenly, you get the joke
you have been playing on yourself.

Da Love-Ananda has often likened this understanding to
the discovery that we have been pinching ourselves. The
function of Da Love-Ananda's Teaching Argument is to alert us
to this activity. He amusingly describes this situation:

DA LOVE-ANANDA: You are all sitting around here
pinching your ass and describing the pain to me! I
see you pinching your ass, but you are so involved
with the pain and all your subjective ruminations
about it that you do not even realize what you are
doing.

Ultimately I call your attention from this pain and all your subjective gaming about it. I grant you sufficient free attention so that you can see. "Look! Look!" That is when you start laughing. That is the moment of humor. You see what it is. [5]

To be restored to humor by this effective use of the Teaching Argument is what Da Love-Ananda calls "hearing". Hearing is a breakthrough of intuitive insight that undoes the self-contraction in the moment. However, a moment's hearing is not sufficient to free one from self-contraction in any ultimate sense. The habit of Narcissus is strong, and we inevitably (and, in most cases, very quickly) turn our face toward the pond again, curling in upon ourselves and creating the pinch of self-possession. We must "hear" again in the next moment, once more penetrating the activity of Narcissus.

For those who are beginning to ponder this Teaching on self-understanding, as well as for those in whom hearing has taken hold as a living process, Da Love-Ananda offers the practice of self-enquiry, or pondering the question "Avoiding relationship?" which summarizes the central Argument of Da Love-Ananda's Wisdom-Teaching. This simple and extremely useful practice was Empowered by Da Love-Ananda during his own ordeal of Realization. When applied either meditatively or randomly during the day, self-enquiry (or relational enquiry, as he has also termed it) is a potent aid in awakening hearing and in keeping the process of hearing alive. In *The Dawn Horse Testament* Da Love-Ananda offers this powerful spiritual practice to Friends and supporters of The Free Daist Communion, as well as to students and practitioners.

As Soon As It Is Truly Understood That self-Contraction Is The Motivating Pain Of life, It Becomes Possible In every moment To Enquire Into (In The Form "Avoiding Relationship?") and Feel Beyond the self-Contraction, and Thus To Enjoy A Native Sense Of Freedom, Well-Being, and Fullness Of Being. [6]

Through present self-understanding and self-transcendence, you awaken in the moment directly to the intuition of native Happiness. And this intuition of Happiness, rather than the search or any "problem", is the radical foundation of the Way that has been Revealed by Da Love-Ananda. This direct approach is perhaps the most outstanding characteristic of the Way of the Heart. From the very beginning, the Way is founded in the Enlightened point of view.

CHAPTER FIVE

Ignorance Is Bliss

In addition to his Teaching Argument about Narcissus, self-understanding, and self-transcendence, Da Love-Ananda has given another essential Argument that is particularly useful for those who are beginning to ponder the Way of the Heart: the Argument of Divine Ignorance.

You have probably experienced moments of wonder and awe, those marvelous occasions when your burden of knowledge dropped away and you were left free, vulnerable, and astounded. Perhaps you were confronted with a natural scene that awakened your sense of infinity, like the ocean or the night sky, or something unutterably beautiful, like a magnificent sunset or the view from a mountaintop, or falling in love. Or such wonder may have come upon you completely unexpectedly. One of Da Love-Ananda's devotees recalls one such surprising revelation:

> Not long ago I was shaving before my bathroom mirror when I noticed, lurking unsuspected in my left sideburn, a clump of grey hairs. I was startled. I was sure they had not been there the day before. Suddenly, I was confronted with the stark evidence that I am growing old. And, of course, it led me to consider that one day I will die. The shock of that recognition swept through my mind like

an eraser over a crowded chalkboard. My thoughts and conceptions were wiped away in an instant, and I was left with the simple feeling of being alive.

My mere existence, the mere existence of anything, was utterly amazing to me. I felt radiantly happy. I was alive and permeated by life, standing astonished in a world that is overflowing with life. I was adrift on the Current of Life, and I had no idea where it would carry me. Nor did I care. I felt no need to know anything. Life itself, mysterious and open-ended as it is, was clearly a happy, conscious, and intelligent process. The sense of wonder that flooded my being carried its own wisdom.

Such moments are glimpses of what Da Love-Ananda calls Divine Ignorance. The mind falls still, lets go of the compartmentalized knowledge by which it armors itself against infinity, and we intuit the unquenchable Mystery of existence.

Da Love-Ananda's Argument is simple and elegant: Consider any object that arises to your attention, whether it is a thought or a thing or a person or an event. Do you know what it is? Really consider it. Don't just sum it up with a name or a bit of language, but allow yourself to see it freshly. What is it?

Consider The Letter "M", For Example. Picture It In mind, or In print, or Write It Down By hand, Even many times. Consider All That You (As the psychophysical self) experience or know About The Letter "M". Do You (in mind or in body) experience or know What The Letter "M" Is? Is? Altogether and Really Is?[1]

We can know all kinds of details about things and events, but we can never know what they are. You may feel as though you know something, but what is that feeling? What is it? What is a thought? How could thinking arise at all? Where does a thought arise? Where is any place? We can locate ourselves in relation to other places, but where are they? Where are we altogether? What is this? We simply do not know.

If you allow this Argument to take effect, if you allow this feeling of not knowing to become conclusive, the mind will come to rest, and you will be restored to Wonder, your natural state. This glimpse of the Mystery of existence opens the being to the Happiness of our natural Condition. As you continue to consider the Argument, you will find that it is deceptively simple—in fact, it is so simple that it is impossible to grasp. It eludes the mind, foiling our habitual defenses against the Unknown. Its simplicity hides a profundity.

Heart-Master Da Love-Ananda's Argument of Divine Ignorance is given to beginners as a means of falling into the inexpressible Mystery of the moment. But to have more than a glimpse of this profundity, to begin to live in that Wonder, requires the real ordeal of self-transcending spiritual practice.

In truth, we <u>never</u> know what anything is. The Unknown—not that which is not yet known, but the Unknowable—is our native State. But to remain in this Mystery, we must be utterly free of the ego's motive to defend itself by seeking knowledge. Otherwise, the moment quickly breaks, and all too soon we return to the presumption of "I", the knower. A student once questioned Da Love-Ananda about the weakness of her ability to feel the Mystery of existence:

DEVOTEE: Why is the feeling of knowing more overwhelming than the feeling of Divine Ignorance?

DA LOVE-ANANDA: Because you are concentrating on it. If you concentrated on the feeling of your foot, it would become overwhelming, too. You still would not know what it is, however. There is simply the contraction, the intensity of conception in any moment, and you do not know what it is. Whatever appears, you do not know what it is. Reduce it to the most fragmentary dispositon of the being—you still do not know what that is. Spiritual practice is to persist in that Divine Ignorance, to examine everything in this moment, and in the next moment.

Believe it or not, it is true that you do not know what a single thing is. That fact remains true, whether you can believe in the effects of the presumption or not. It is always true. In as many moments as you return to it, it is true. Return to it fifty times a decade, it is true those fifty times. Return to it three times a day, it is true three times a day. Return to it every five minutes, it is true that often. Return to it perpetually, every second, it is true that often. Return to it tacitly, so that you need not even return, so that it is <u>simply</u> true, and it is all that is true.

God, the unspeakable, is in our midst and is the Domain of all our existence. This Truth is all that any Adept has ever pointed to. The difference is that the Adept has Realized this disposition by persistence, while you only make contact with it in a moment and then flash back into your conventional state.

You realize you cannot persist in the Argument from moment to moment. The Argument is simply true, but persisting in it from moment to moment is what God-Realization is all about. No being can do it. It is God's business. It is completely a matter of Grace. No will can persist in it. You will drive yourself insane if you try to do it. All you can do is hear it. Be sympathetic to the point of presuming the discipline, then enter into the Company of the Agency that communicates it to you, and be submissive, whole bodily, in that Company. That, too, is difficult. The whole thing is difficult. Life is difficult in any case. Even if you do not take up this Way, you will suffer and die. Where are you all going? You are going to be dead in a few years, so why not submit yourself to what is obviously true with as much energy as you can summon? Then see what you realize. [2]

CHAPTER SIX

No Practice Realizes Truth

a talk by Heart-Master Da Love-Ananda
October 19, 1977

)A LOVE-ANANDA: Finding ourselves alive in an independent
form, vulnerable and subject to death, we become fright-
ied, afraid of extinction. This fearful mood motivates us in
l that we hope, believe, and do. We seek the consolation that
e will continue in the face of the threat of death. This urge
)r consolation enters into all of our considerations. Any
elief in our own continuation after death is created in our
eed to be consoled. Thus, if we are to discover the destiny
eyond physical death, we must first of all become free of the
emand for consolation that causes us merely to believe
ther than to inspect, to understand and be free. Otherwise,
e could never be certain that we are not just believing
ecause we are afraid. We cannot be certain of our own
)iritual or religious hopes and beliefs unless we are com-
etely free of the need to be consoled. We might observe
)mething about life that implies continuation after death, but
e cannot be certain so long as we feel compelled to believe
as a consolation for our fear.

Fear is projected on all our experience, but it is not itself
herent in all things. It is a characteristic of our usual
)ndition that we project on all our experience and circum-
ance. Examine it as your experience itself and see if fear is
herent in all things or if it is a characteristic of your own
)nsciousness that is unnecessary. There is no information

that can liberate you from it, because our whole involvement with information and knowledge is secondary to fear itself. Thus, freedom from fear is based on a fundamental liberation that occurs prior to all external causes. You cannot even talk about the Divine in any sense that is fully satisfying, happy, and free until you are already free of fear. Belief in God is not the way to become free of fear. It is merely consolation. If we are to enjoy Communion with God, we must be free of fear already.

We become free of fear by abiding in our native or prior Condition, not imploded, not engaged in the reaction that is fear. Thus, rather than projecting that contraction on all our experience, we exist as love, effortless, unobstructed feeling. Usually all our effort is a response to the sense of fear and the aggravation of experience. But from the point of view of love, which is not fear, we are no longer in need of consolation. We may simply be satisfied in our ordinary relations then. And we may be free to observe the conditions of existence, of experience, of knowledge.

Now this is a different matter altogether from assuming that you can become free of fear merely by thinking about it, by analyzing it. People like to think that, in a moment of reflection, they can become completely free of fear. One well-known spiritual philosopher continually tells his casual audiences that they can become "completely free of fear!" in the course of an evening's consideration. You are simply to sit there and think about it, and then when you leave the auditorium you will be "completely free of fear!" You all like this idea of going inside, working on yourselves, being philosophical, or thinking things through, and believing that such activity is supposed to be or lead to salvation and happiness and freedom. But the spiritual demand is a moral demand. There is no freedom from fear until you live a life of love. There is no freedom until subjectivity or mere consideration becomes incident, new adaptation, a new practice of life. Literal love, which feels beyond all the limiting forces of experience, is the highest and most necessary philosophical activity or process. In that case you observe that you are already completely free of fear, whereas mere thought is self-meditation and a strategy in dilemma, fear, and lovelessness.

You cannot become free of fear through mere philosophical or subjective reflection. That is total nonsense. Fear arises in our contraction, our withdrawal from the pattern of our relations, our separation from Infinity. The spiritual demand is not, "Think about all of that and then it will not be true, and you will not have to be afraid anymore." The spiritual communication is a demand for a moral transformation of your whole existence, your whole life. You cannot be free of fear just by sitting here thinking about it or reading a book. You must consider the mechanism of fear, yes, but then you must go and serve and work and love and be transformed, newly adapted. You must live a life in which fear, the mood of contraction, is made obsolete by love, which is feeling-attention to Infinity. No discussion in a hall or from an armchair completely relieves you of fear or of any problems you might have in life, including your compulsive thinking mind. All of these things that you are suffering are expressions of one affair, this contraction of the whole body-being, the contraction of feeling-attention, the collapse on oneself. That is the whole matter. And to be free of it we must begin to live differently. Simply to think about and consider freedom may make it sound good here and now, but that subjective activity does not change anything fundamentally. Even in that case, you are still everything that your past adaptation makes you.

So you must go and live differently—and it is very difficult to live differently! Only our insight, our responsiveness to the Spiritual Master, our enjoyment of the Grace of the Divine, makes living differently tolerable. Only Divine Communion makes us able to pass through the moments when we are tending to return to our previous state, to the consolations of our childishness. So whatever is wrong with anybody, whatever is troubling you, it is a matter of whether you love or not. The things that are wrong with you are expressions of your contraction of feeling-attention. When you are feeling good, it is because you are not exercising this recoil so profoundly as when you are feeling bad. But to get rid of the recoil a little bit is not sufficient. That is not spiritual life. That might be sufficient to improve your ordinary middle-class life, but it is

not sufficient for true spiritual Realization, Happiness altogether, which is a profoundly creative process.

The fundamental Principle of our existence is to persist as
love, as Radiance prior to fear. Love is the fundamental Condition. Everything else is secondary to it, mere experience to be
met either by fear or love, by contracting upon ourselves or
radiating in all relations to Infinity. As long as we are not love,
then every moment is a problem, a dilemma, in which we try
to manipulate the circumstances of experience in order to
console ourselves. But all our experience is distorted, all our
relations are corrupted, everything fails to satisfy. Thus, we
look for beliefs of all kinds, because we are afraid, unsatisfied,
and unconsoled.

You cannot truly enter into spiritual life in order to be
consoled, to be relieved from fear. But that is exactly why the
usual man engages spiritual practice, in order to attain the
goal of bliss, or release from fear, or immortality. The search
for happiness is not the position from which to enter truly
into spiritual life. You must approach God as a devotee,
already blissful, already free of fear, already alive as love.
Therefore, come to me when you are already happy.

This is the secret of spiritual life: Love is God-Communion, or freedom from fear. The inherent disposition of Radiance is God-Communion, presently God-Communion, in this
moment. No objective experience, no vision, no esoteric
structure or condition of any kind is God-Realization, nor does
any experience or condition add to this Communion. The path
itself is to be love, to be unobstructed feeling-attention, to
persist in love under all conditions, and thereby to transform
the conditions of existence from that point of view. If we
abide in that Communion, then all conditions and possibilities
of existence are a great display of God that will always be
benign.

But regardless of the experience, high or low, there is
always one single, dominant Principle, one great and fundamental Significance. It is the same Principle that you must
continuously realize as your responsibility apart from all
else. Everything else is merely an emanation of it, an elabora-
tion that does not in any sense qualify this fundamental

responsibility.

In *The Knee of Listening* I described it as "understanding". It is the same as Love, unobstructed feeling-attention, God-Communion. If you will adhere to it, you need not be concerned for any complexity of experience. Experience is altogether without significance. Not a single vision or experience adds to God-Communion. All experience only realizes a lesser destiny than the Destiny of God-Communion, which moves not to heavens but directly to God in every moment. Therefore, in every moment we must be responsible for God-Communion, for moving beyond the contraction of feeling-attention, the avoidance of relationship, the contraction that is the ego, the falling into the principal mood of fear and thereby experiencing existence as a dilemma, as a search for consolation that never ends and that is never satisfied.

The spiritual traditions are filled with doctrines of practice and esoteric knowledge, which are assumed to be necessary and leading to God. Thus, people think that their spiritual life is the practice of methodical and strategic approaches that lead through this life, through many lives perhaps, to the ultimate moment, the ultimate hope. But all such practice is fruitless. No knowledge is God. Even the traditional path of devotion, wherein you work yourself into a fierce state of emotional ecstasy for God, does not realize God.

No practice realizes Truth. Truth is realized through the inspection of experience to the point of realizing that experience has no obligatory force and that none of it is the point of spiritual !ife. The point is this single responsibility, this single principle, this single inspection of your state in this moment, of your self-concern, of the contraction toward fear. Be responsible for that contraction so that you exist instead as Love, or God-Communion. That is everything. That is the whole Teaching.

There is nothing to be attained. There is a single principle for which we must be responsible, and that is God-Realization. It is not the <u>way</u> to God-Realization. It is God-Realization itself. It is the disposition in Truth. It is the Way of life. Once it is Realized, nothing else obliges us. In itself it is not a matter of any vision, any esoteric or worldly experience. All conditions, if they do arise, are undermined by the force of God-Communion and are no longer obligatory, no longer your destiny. You pass right through them.

There is only one discipline: to become responsible for the contraction of feeling-attention by moving beyond fear in every moment into the disposition of love. It is the only discipline. If you will hear this, you do not have to do anything else. Live this process with me and it is always the same. It does not itself grow or change. It is simple, direct, absolute.

This, then, is the ultimate consideration of spiritual life. It always has been. In Krishna's argument to Arjuna in the *Bhagavad Gita,* Krishna reveals all the esoteric matters to his devotee, and then he tells him that they are not truth. He brings Arjuna to the point of understanding the fruitlessness of the whole affair of ordinary life and spiritual seeking. And then he communicates to him the essential Process, which is not strategically to turn the ego, or the contraction that is fear, toward various kinds of subjective and objective conditions and methods. On the contrary, Krishna tells Arjuna to "abandon all dharmas"—not only all duties, but all teachings, all philosophies, all supports, all methods, all approaches, all meditation and contemplation, all esotericism, all consolations in the world, all ways of trying to be fulfilled in the world, all ways of trying to examine the conditions of life in order to feel that they are all right—and he tells him, "Turn to Me. Abandon all supports and turn to Me. Remember Me. Meditate on Me. Remember Me and fight." Go back, change everything entirely on the basis of this Remembrance, this Communion with Me. Not "Me" in terms of the independent man Krishna, or even his subtle form as it might appear in visions or dreams, but the "Me" that is God, the Spiritual Master in Truth, alive as Love itself.

Love is God-Communion, and that is the whole path. Live it under all conditions. If you live by that principle, you change everything. Fear is a way of creating and solidifying everything. Fear is the ego. From the point of view of the ego we create all of our experience. The ego is projected on all of our experience, all of our human relations, all of our esoteric relations. Everything we do is an expression of that egoic dilemma. Therefore, the way to change everything is not to take up the position of fear or the egoic dilemma any longer, but to be love, to live in God-Communion. Then you will also continue your experience. Whatever arises and involves you in the ordinary way, you will live from the point of view of this principle, and on its basis transform the conditions of existence. Your life will be a manifestation of God-Communion then. That is the simple affair. That is all there is to it.

Jesus said the same thing very plainly. When people asked him casually, he would tell them the whole way right there in a moment—love God and be love in all your relations. That is it. There is nothing else to do. There is nothing else to realize. There is not a single experience that will add to it. That is the whole Realization. It is the whole Way. God is not at the end of it, but "the Father and I are one". This is not just true of Jesus, it is true of everyone. It is the Truth of everything.

You must live from the point of view of that Truth. Such a life is Divine. The Divine life is not an effort toward the realization of Truth. It is to live already in Truth. It is the Principle of life. I do not know how to make it any more plain!

SECTION THREE

THE
HEART-MASTER

The Perfect Teachers of Man are the Transcendental Adepts. They appear in various times and places, to Awaken all individual beings to the Living Divine and to create a renewal of truly human and spiritual culture. They unanimously declare and confess that only the Living God, the Eternally Radiant Divine Being in whom all beings and things arise and inhere, is the Truth and Ever-Present Savior of Man. The Adepts come and go. They Serve and Incarnate the One who is always already here.

Da Love-Ananda
Scientific Proof of the Existence
of God Will Soon Be Announced
by the White House! *p. 300*

1986

CHAPTER SEVEN

"No Fish Is to Die"

by Jeff Polson

When I returned from the Vietnam War in 1968, I immediately became engrossed in an intense spiritual search. For three years I read *The Tibetan Book of the Dead* over and over again, with the result that my search became more and more desperate. At last I undertook an ordeal in which I climbed a mountain in Oregon, chanting every inch of the way, fully expecting to receive a great revelation when I reached the top. But nothing happened. My whole search seemed dead. The scriptures I was reading were dead. And most of all, my heart was dead. I came to the conclusion that I needed a Spiritual Master, and a week or two later I discovered *The Knee of Listening*, Da Love-Ananda's spiritual autobiography. I joined the Communion in September 1974.

In late fall of 1978 I was asked to set up a fish tank in Da Love-Ananda's residence. I was overjoyed at the opportunity to perform this service. In my enthusiasm, I replied that I knew "all about" fish and aquariums, having had vast experience in the field. Actually, I had only kept a twenty-gallon tank for about a year with a few small tropical fish!

I jumped right in. I immediately bought a fifty-five gallon aquarium with all the necessary accoutrements, which I installed in Da Love-Ananda's residence. When I was finished, I received a message from Da Love-Ananda: "No fish is to die."

No fish is to die?! I thought back on the number of fish

that had perished in my limited and brief career. I had pulled many lifeless bodies from the water. Everybody who has kept fish has lost fish. I was taken aback, but I acknowledged (although doubtfully) this mandate.

Shortly after the first tank was placed in Da Love-Ananda's residence, I added another, then another, then two more. Before long there were nine tanks (marine, tropical, and goldfish) in his residence under my care. Needless to say, the casualties were soon to begin.

Indeed, it was not long at all before I was called over to the house to remove a dead fish from one of the tanks—the first of many. I was told that Da Love-Ananda wanted to know why he had died. I took the two-inch corpse in hand and studied it—no wounds, no signs of disease or distress. In fact, it was still quite beautiful. But it was dead. I replied that I didn't know why.

As the days passed, there were more sick fish and more deaths. I became proficient at spotting diseases and learning how to minister to the victims. Nonetheless, many fish continued to perish.

One day I was called to tend to yet another sick fish. I went to Da Love-Ananda's residence to find a dwarf gourami floating on the surface of the tank, his body already frozen in a rigid arc, indicating death was near. I was told that Da Love-Ananda wanted me to "save this fish."

"Save this fish?" I thought. "Nothing can save this fish!"

Still, I removed him from the tank and took him to a hospital tank in my home. There I treated the water with medication. I watched him for a few minutes, hoping that there would be some sign that he would recover. I placed a hand on either side of the tank and prayed for him. I also poured in a small amount of holy water—water that has been infused with the healing energy that is Radiant in Da Love-Ananda's spiritual Company and in the holy sites that he has Empowered as his Agencies. But the moment I had seen him, I had known that the fish would not survive. In twenty minutes he was dead.

I took his body from the tank and flushed it down the toilet.

A devotee, who had come to my house, had been watching while I tended to the fish. After I had disposed of the gourami, I said, "Well, there goes another one."

He looked at me. "Don't you feel anything for him?" he asked.

"No," I said, "it's just a fish. Do you?"

"Yes!"

"You do?" I was really surprised.

"Yes!"

"Do you think most people would?"

"Yes!"

This was a revelation to me. I had felt nothing for these fish. I had no emotional connection to them. That was the point—I felt no emotion. I had approached the matter intelligently and with a good deal of energy. But I didn't care about their lives. I hadn't given my heart. And I saw that it wasn't just fish this lesson was about. It was an indication of how I live my life.

The following day Da Love-Ananda asked how the fish was doing. I realized that he had truly expected the fish to be healed. I saw that I would have to engage this service in a new way. And I got a message from Da Love-Ananda:

"You should do everything possible to save the fish. Find out everything you can, do everything you can to heal them. When you have done it all, then go to the Communion Hall, and pray."

I should interject here that I did not take lightly Da Love-Ananda's mandate that there should be no dead fish. I was constantly studying the subject, reading books, talking to experienced aquarists, university professors, and anyone else I thought could help. But now I intensified this study.

Before long, I was called to the house again. A fish was "acting funny" in one of the marine tanks. It was a blue-faced angel, one of my favorites. When I had first begun setting up aquariums for Da Love-Ananda, I was taken by the beauty of this fish, and I immediately decided to buy the fish as a gift for Da Love-Ananda. But blue-faced angels are so delicate that I had to wait many months, allowing the tank environment to stabilize completely, before I felt it was possible to present Da

Love-Ananda with this gift. So when this particular fish took ill, I felt a real desire to keep it alive. I am certain that Da Love-Ananda intuitively felt my connection to this fish, because he took a strong interest in its welfare, examining it with me when I went to his residence to check on its condition.

The diagnosis and treatment of fish diseases is a little-researched and inexact science. Many times the symptoms are not specific enough to indicate a treatment. Quite often any treatment is a shot in the dark.

I elected to leave the angel in the tank. Movement of a fish causes stress, often worsening the condition of one already ailing. I treated the tank with a wide-spectrum anti-biotic, and then I went to the Communion Hall to pray for him.

I breathed to my heart and asked Da Love-Ananda to come to his aid. I felt how I wanted him to live. I stayed in the Communion Hall for an hour and a half.

Throughout the day I kept my attention on the fish, at the same time feeling Da Love-Ananda with my heart, and directing toward the fish the healing energy contacted through my Communion with Da Love-Ananda. That evening I returned to the house to observe the patient again. His condition had worsened. I decided to move him to a tank in my home.

I placed him in a hospital tank and added a small amount of holy water and a bit of holy ash—a pure white ash remaining from a fire ceremony performed at one of the holy sites. I again placed my hands on either side of the tank and prayed. His condition worsened. As he weakened, I put my hand in the water and gently cradled him, praying for him. I was filled with compassion for that being, and I stayed with him until he died at three the following morning. Then I took his body to a pond on the Sanctuary, said a prayer, and threw him into the water.

The next day I was with Da Love-Ananda at his residence. He asked how the angel was. I told him that he had died. It was hard to give him this news, because I had really felt the loss of the fish. Da Love-Ananda looked at me and quietly spoke, "It was his time." I don't know what I expected, but I didn't expect that response. I was at once perplexed and undone by Da Love-Ananda's compassion and gentleness.

There was no miraculous recovery to thrill me, but I had learned how to bring life to another, how to serve death, and what it means to be feelingly present in doing both. I am grateful forever to Da Love-Ananda for his instruction and his endless Grace. Every moment in his spiritual Company is Revelation.

CHAPTER EIGHT

The Hero of the Heart

Martians in Texas and the Ultimate Taboo

Suppose one day you read the following headline:

ALIEN SPACECRAFT FOUND IN TEXAS
SEARCH LAUNCHED FOR "ET" PILOT

How will you react? Will you be skeptical? Afraid? Awed? Excited? Will your mind leap to consider the consequences of this event—for yourself, and for humanity as a whole?

Now suppose the headline reads:

MINNESOTA RESIDENT CLAIMS IDENTITY
WITH DIVINE BEING
URGES ALL TO PRACTICE SPIRITUAL LIFE

But this is hardly a believable headline. It seems pretty unlikely that our Minnesotan resident would be considered front page news.

But why not? Let's rephrase the headline to highlight the importance of the event:

ENGLISHMAN DISCOVERS MEANS FOR ALL
TO KNOW ETERNAL BOUNDLESS HAPPINESS

No, this is still not a believable headline.

Why not? Why would it seem more newsworthy, important, and universally relevant that aliens from outer space might land in Texas than that a Minnesotan or an Englishman might Realize unconditional Happiness and be able to lead others to that same Realization?

Perhaps such "good news" is just too unbelievable. Compared to the landing of Martians in Texas, the Realization of infinite Bliss may be a far more stupendous event. The flight of alien beings through space is an achievement we can conceive of within our ordinary understanding of the universe. But to transcend the boundaries of "I"—to Realize Identity with the One Being that is the source and substance of all beings and things—is literally inconceivable. It cannot be grasped by the mind. Therefore, it is utterly "unreasonable".

And because such Realization goes beyond every convention by which we act and think, it is the ultimate taboo. Generally today people feel free to <u>seek</u> God or to <u>worship</u> whatever God they choose. But to <u>Realize</u> God, to proclaim the Bliss of God-Realization, is strictly taboo.

DA LOVE-ANANDA: A cultic object is allowed to be Divine in this world, a God in a book is allowed to be Divine, all kinds of fetishes are allowed to be Divine, but you are not allowed to be Divine! You are allowed to worship cultic objects and assume them to be Divine, but you cannot become Divine.

You have ceased to be unreasonable. You have ceased to live in your fundamental and prior Condition, which is Enjoyment, Bliss, Happiness.

The Divine is infinitely Present, perfectly, absolutely and eternally Present, and available. The Divine must be lived, not sought. The Divine is the Condition of the world, not the ultimate hope of the world. There is no hope whatsoever. If the Divine is not <u>presently</u> lived, there is no Second Coming, no Millenium, no Revelation, no Liberation, no Nirvana. But if men began to live the Truth, if men became capable of ecstasy in society with one another, you would see a vast and immediate transformation of the world.[1]

The Hero of the Heart

The history of Heart-Master Da Love-Ananda's life and Work is the account of one who has dared to break the ultimate taboo and to live the Happiness of Realization to others. Da Love-Ananda is the most paradoxical of men—he displays simultaneously the qualities of vulnerable human love and Divine Realization. A practitioner describes one of countless incidents in which Da Love-Ananda has touched the hearts of his devotees, demonstrating the great Love he feels for everyone.

> Once, in March 1984, I was part of a small group invited to a formal question and answer occasion at Da Love-Ananda's residence. In that personal setting he inundated his devotees with his great Love. The room was afloat in his Heart-Radiance. At one point, devotees began to speak of their love for him. Uncharacteristically, I also spoke up, expressing my gratitude for the many Blessings I had been given. As I opened my mouth to speak, Da Love-Ananda turned his gaze full upon me.
>
> In an instant, all self-consciousness fell away as I looked into the eyes of Love Itself. His face was broken by Love, its every line and contour molded by compassion. His expression was completely open, full of human understanding and heartbreaking vulnerability. It hardly mattered what words I said—we were transported to another realm where only Love is spoken. He drew my love from me, and for a timeless moment I was able to be completely, openly loving, without thought, without reservation or embarrassment. I was filled with a Love so great that there was no room left over for any thought of "self".

He had transformed what had begun as my urge to give him my love into his Gift to me, drawing me beyond myself and showing me how it feels to be Love only.

This Love is Da Love-Ananda's most outstanding characteristic. People commonly think that to be Enlightened is to become immune to human emotion, living in a state of invulnerable tranquility. But Enlightenment is the fullest expression of humanity, and thus it is the demonstration of the most profound of human emotions—Love:

DA LOVE-ANANDA: The ego-transcending point of view actively acknowledges the principle of love. The individual who is either Enlightened or is functioning in an ego-transcending fashion presumes himself or herself to live in a world of love. In the world of relations, that one is alive in the Domain of Love. Love is the principle of functioning. It is the principle of relationship. Love is what is to be realized and expressed. You must overcome all limits upon it. Spiritual life is many things, but at the level of human relations, its essence is love.

You have rather abstract notions about the state of the Spiritual Master. You tend to think that the Spiritual Master is somehow exclusively a transcendental state and that this human machine sits out here and helps people out and deals with their tendencies. But that is not the way it is. I personally (and anyone who functions as Spiritual Master) am not someone who does not love. How could it be imagined that that is so? Yet, you conceive of me in merely abstract terms rather than in the fullest possible terms. It is egos that have trouble with love and cannot love, while Spiritual Masters have no defenses against unlove and are completely involved in loving.

If devotees are to use me spiritually, they must know that I love them. They must be absolutely certain of it. They must know it is true of me humanly.

Spiritual Realization, Spiritual Adeptship, is a human demonstration. There is nothing about being a Spiritual Master that is not human. To be a Spiritual Master is profoundly human, the fullest Realization of being human. Spiritual Masters or Awakened beings, truly free, exhibit the most human sign of Love. [2]

Because the Heart-Master has no defenses against our unlove, his Work with devotees is the evidence of a Love that is heroic in its manifestation. Having passed through the great ordeal of Realization himself, his life is dedicated to serving others for the sake of their Realization. He willingly undertakes any trial in order to set Free those who are bound by the chains of the ego. The tremendously difficult life of the Heart-Master requires the character and the courage of a great spiritual Warrior, a hero of the Heart. Da Love-Ananda has spoken of the overwhelming struggle that the Adept must go through:

DA LOVE-ANANDA: You must understand that the unique status of the Spiritual Master is not given for his own sake. The Spiritual Master is not a human being with a superior egoic consciousness that he or she is God. The ego of such a one is transcended in the process of his or her lifetime. The situation of the Spiritual Master is not as you might imagine. You may be thinking: "We all know you are not suffering like us! We poor bastards are the ones who are suffering— you've got it made!" Well, such thinking is not true at all. The lifetime of the Spiritual Master is only sacrifice, and therefore more a torment than the lifetime of the ordinary soul. Read the biographies of the great Spiritual Masters. They all tell the same story of a life that is terrible in some ways, a life in which frequently they are exploited and rejected, and in which they are under the constant threat of domination by worldly and negative forces. Such individuals are always dealing with great forces, not just mastering their rejection by human beings. Such is also the case in my lifetime!

Understand this: No un-Enlightened soul wants to be in the position of the Spiritual Master! If you understood my constant experience, you would not envy it—nor could you endure it! One must be Helped by a great Divine Power in order to endure the events associated with such a unique life, in order to pass through such events with a clear understanding of what they are as a Divine Process. Only the Divine has the power to endure the complete revolution of consciousness. [3]

Da Love-Ananda does not merely communicate <u>about</u> Enlightenment. He awakens the direct intuition of that Freedom and Happiness. If you are willing to truly give your attention to what Da Love-Ananda has to say, you will come to feel the force of the Adept's Teaching Argument in your own life. And if you persist in your consideration, you will also come to intuit the Happiness that is Da Love-Ananda's constant and tangible communication.

Da Love-Ananda's Wisdom-Teaching is not and never has been intended for mere intellectual persuasion or belief. Mere belief in some great figure or in some esoteric truth may be comforting, giving one hope in a dark hour. But, as everyone discovers sooner or later, mere belief is not enough to make anyone truly Happy. Authentic spiritual life requires you to transcend the greatest of all obstacles—your self, or ego. For that, you must come to a real understanding of yourself, an understanding profound enough to penetrate your superficial self-image and lay bare the aspects of your character that you would prefer not to notice. And beyond that, you must come to see the root action that is the ego, the action by which you actually prevent true Happiness. Through that understanding, you begin to intuit the Happiness that has always been available to you and that is, in fact, your native Condition.

Da Love-Ananda is the first to criticize, and in the strongest terms, any response to him that is based on blind belief:

DA LOVE-ANANDA: I have made it very clear that the Teaching, which I have communicated openly, is not given so that you will believe it. I am not interested in involving myself in any manipulative techniques merely to create belief-mind in you.

At first, simply listen to my Arguments and respond. My confession of Realization will be true for you as your spiritual life and your recognition of me develop. Then my own confession becomes, in effect, your confession. You know it to be so, not because you have become involved in belief-mind, the mere conditioning of yourself as an ego, but because you have gone beyond the egoic limitations and have entered into the domain of real spiritual practice. [4]

And again:

DA LOVE-ANANDA: I have not realized God by containing God in this skin! It is by transcending this skin and this mind that God has been realized to be absolute and all-pervading, my own Condition. It is not me with a small "m" that is God. This body-mind is not God. God is the Condition of the world. This is my Realization, which I can proclaim to you.

In the midst of that Realization, this body-mind achieves an uncommon function, as is the case for anyone who matures in the higher aspects of spiritual life. An incomparable Radiance communicates through that person and is felt by others. That is the Radiance of God—no doubt!—and it does not have its position, its origin and its limiting identity, inside that person you see before you. If I alone am God, then whenever I leave the room, you are separated from God. How absurd! [5]

CHAPTER NINE

"Play from the Point of View of God!"

by Byron Duckwall

A t seven I began my study of music by learning to play the cello. I was taught by my father, a life-long professional musician and successful music teacher. At age eight I started piano lessons, and a year later I began studying music at the university nearby. I studied composition, went to special music camps, and won competitions.

By the time I was thirteen I was committed to a life's pursuit of artistic excellence. I sacrificed much to develop my music, practicing long hours, giving up athletics, social occasions, sometimes even friends. And I was constantly confronted with the intense frustration of this effort.

Out of this ordeal has grown a real passion and love of music, and a professional career in music, but also a great obsession. In the early 1970s I was working for the Metropolitan Opera Association, playing frequent concerts in the U.S. (in places such as Lincoln Center and Carnegie Hall) and abroad (including Brazil,where I was first cello in the Orcestra Estadual do Sao Paulo). I was always working to forge my artistry.

But while I developed as a musician, I began to have a peculiar feeling that this great passion and love for music would not be the sum total of my life. Even as a child I had an intuition, which became stronger in my late teens, that something was going to enter my life that would change it completely. I did not know what it would be, but I knew that I would give myself to it totally.

In 1974 a friend of mine called me late one night and excitedly praised a man named Franklin Jones (Da Love-Ananda's given name). I was attracted to something I sensed in my friend's communication that was different from his usual talk. He sent me a copy of *The Knee of Listening.* I loved this book so much that I would not part with it even when I slept. While I was reading it, I had experiences of forceful energies and feelings of love. I felt an uncommon sympathy with this biography of Da Love-Ananda. So I decided to write a letter to him. In that letter, quite spontaneously and to my surprise, a deep passion began pouring out. I even said in the letter that I did not understand why I was expressing my deepest feelings to him, except that it felt very important to me. I pleaded with Da Love-Ananda to not disregard this letter but to respond to it because it was very important to me.

Little did I realize how fast the Guru responds to the heart of his devotee. That night in a dream, Da Love-Ananda told me that I should come and see him right away, and that all of the practical matters that I was worried about would work themselves out naturally. He told me that I should just relax and come as quickly as possible.

Within a day I had made all of the necessary arrangements and was on a cross-country bus headed for California, where Da Love-Ananda lived at the time. In my diary I wrote that I felt I had embarked upon the great adventure of my life. Shortly thereafter I met Da Love-Ananda.

Nearly two years passed. During this time I was involved in Da Love-Ananda's historic Teaching Demonstrations, while living in the community of students and practitioners who surrounded him. These were wonderful, albeit difficult, times for me. A great learning process was taking place on every level of my being.

In 1976 I offered to play for the Heart-Master as part of the program for a major celebration. I rehearsed for weeks, wanting to do my very best. Secretly, I worried that I would not be good enough, and when the day of the celebration came, I was quite anxious. It seemed to me to be the most important performance I had ever given.

I had prepared two works. After the first piece, the audience applauded enthusiastically, and I plunged into the next work, much relieved. The second performance was also going quite well. I was really "on" and excited to be playing so proficiently. But about halfway through the solo, several loud explosions brought my playing to an abrupt end. Someone had tossed a lighted string of firecrackers at me and my cello! I was disoriented by the noise and felt confused, angry, and helpless at the interruption. I was totally offended that some ill-mannered crazy person had done this to me.

But then the stage manager waved me off stage, and I listened, still dazed, as he informed me that it was the Heart-Master who had thrown the firecrackers at me and my cello! More perplexed and bewildered than ever, I wondered, "I know he loves me. Why would he do this to me?"

As Grace would have it, while working at the Communion's bookstore in San Francisco a few nights later, I was invited with another musician to play again for Da Love-Ananda. This time the Heart-Master asked me to finish the piece that had been interrupted by the firecrackers. I played what I could remember of it, but my playing was not very good. My timing was off and my performance was limp. Da Love-Ananda laughed at my attempt and said, "You really can't stop showing off, can you?" Then he took my cello like a violin under his chin and pretended to play it. (Since then, Da Love-Ananda has blessed my cello by handling it on several occasions. The instrument actually played differently after he touched it.)

I was invited to stay for dinner with Da Love-Ananda that night, which was a great honor for me. As I moved to take my seat at the end of the table, Da Love-Ananda said, "Byron, why don't you come and sit next to me?"

I was ecstatic. During dinner I conversed with Da Love-Ananda and another devotee whom I knew well. As we talked about other devotees and the events of our lives, I was able to ask the Heart-Master some questions I had wanted to ask him. But at the same time a certain frustration began to grow in me.

The seemingly lighthearted nature of the conversation and the circumstance appeared to be preventing me from asking the Heart-Master some deeply personal questions. It was the frustration of being with a God-Realized Being and yet not feeling free to ask him the questions that had troubled me for years.

Suddenly, however, I became aware that two conversations were going on simultaneously. Coincident with the apparent small-talk of the dinner conversation was a silent conversation of the Heart. It was a literal conversation. Though it was not spoken, or even thought in the head, it was as tangible as the usual spoken word. I was happily shocked by this psychic phenomenon, and overwhelmed by the great opportunity it afforded me. My heart flooded out to the Heart-Master as I asked him my most secret, intimate, and heartfelt questions about the nature of existence, true Bliss, and true Ecstasy. Were they what I had always intuited? And in this silent conversation Da Love-Ananda revealed the Happy Truth. I was overwhelmed.

I realized at one point that Da Love-Ananda could not know these questions unless he was me. This thought was amazing to me. And as the thought occurred to me, I looked up at him, and he looked me right in the eye and roared with laughter. Immediately I knew it was true. It was a miracle, a great mystery! And the Adept had revealed it to me with the playfulness of a child, delighting in my revelation. At this point I felt madly in love with him.

Eventually the evening drew to a close, and Da Love-Ananda left. As his car pulled away, I rushed toward it, reached out, and kissed him through the open window, proclaiming my love for him. Da Love-Ananda acknowledged me with "Tcha", his characteristic expression of Blessing, and the car pulled away into the night.

Many years after this event, I reached a point at which I felt moved to make a big change in my life. Spontaneously I decided to begin a long fast as a gesture of renunciation of my egoic tendencies. During the fast, I had a profound experience. One night my father telephoned me. He wanted me to send him some music that we had recently discussed. As I searched through my files, it occurred to me that this was the very piece that I was performing when the Heart-Master had thrown the firecrackers at me. I began to recollect and reflect upon that event once more. I also remembered other incidents with Da Love-Ananda. He had praised my musical service to him. He had threatened to throw water balloons at me while I was performing. He had had me play in an airport. He had once pretended to be a psychotic, mock-attacking me with a butterknife in the midst of a performance! He had broken out into ecstatic speech in the middle of a piece, telling me to let go of my social consciousness and keep my attention in God. He had served me in so many ways!

By pointing out that I always show off when I perform, he immediately put me in touch with all the painful motives of self-seeking underlying my musicianship. By constantly disrupting my performances and jarring me out of self-possession, he helped me to understand myself better and thus awakened me to the Heart. I began to remember many other instances of his serving me, events that had nothing to do with music. I marveled at how perfectly he had reflected me back to myself. He had always been completely in touch with my real feelings.

I sat there amazed. I had been utterly unaware of Da Love-Ananda's great compassion and submission to devotees. Now I felt free. There was no dilemma. I felt my usual limitations, but they did not matter. I began laughing. At that moment, I saw and felt a golden light. This light was coincident with the intuition of freedom I was feeling. I sensed that only from the point of view of this freedom could I or anyone else see or experience this light. It seemed to be Happiness itself and appeared to be coming from the Heart-Master as I looked at a picture of him on the wall of my room. It was coming through an invisible hole in the universe that was miraculously simultaneous with this world. It was as though there were two worlds coincident with each other, one limited and the other absolutely free—as in the silent conversation of the Heart with Da Love-Ananda in 1976.

I stayed awake long into the night contemplating this liberating intuition and the adventure of my relationship with the Heart-Master. I saw that the period following those incidents with Da Love-Ananda had been a time of rapid musical and spiritual growth. It was not an easy time musically because I was constantly thrown up against my limitations. I felt that the Teaching Argument had made its mark in me, and now I was seeing all of its practical applications in my art. I kept feeling that I had run into a brick wall musically. But then I would apply what I had learned from Da Love-Ananda and the Teaching Argument, and that action would take me beyond myself.

At one point I remembered I had hit rock bottom. I had no money, and I could not see any way past some real limitations in my music. Then I remembered that the Heart-Master had written, "If it has become complicated, return to the basics." So I went back to the most basic elements of my craft and began reexamining them in detail.

This was the beginning of a whole new approach to music for me. I met various teachers in New York who helped me, and they were amazed by my rapid development. I made one quantum leap after another in my understanding and performance of music. I was learning things that both my teachers and I thought were impossible for me. I did not feel that "I" was doing it. It was the Heart coming forward. It was a miracle.

In recent years all of these events have come into still clearer perspective for me. During his Teaching Demonstrations, Da Love-Ananda had shocked, coaxed, taunted, jarred, and attracted me out of all my preconceived and conventional ideas of what it is to be a musician. Through his actions, he stripped away my false notions about art, leaving me in a vulnerable position, able to observe my own limitations. Then I began to observe the difference between my conventional or egoic involvement with music and how musically to express the feeling of the Heart that Da Love-Ananda had awakened in me.

In *The Knee of Listening* Da Love-Ananda states:

> Creativity is the idol of the West. All its activities and knowledge, even its obsessions, are a worship of

creativity, the source and force of generation (p. 246).

Creativity is the symbol or meaning of life. No-creation is the symbol or meaning of truth. They are only intuitions of reality itself, which is neither one nor numbered, but coincident with all that appears and is known (p. 246).

Narcissus is an idol of creativity, of source. . . . He is the reduction of the world to the form of his own separate person (p. 254).

I had made creativity rather than Truth or Love my idol. I thought creativity was Happiness. But "I" was always the one being creative—the ego was always active. Thus, even though I sacrificed myself to my art, it remained a limited activity. It was just a grand obsession. I came to realize that present Communion with the Heart or the Spirit was the only way to be free of my egoic obsession with music. I saw that creativity in itself is nothing special. I didn't need my music as a means to attain Happiness—Happiness was, and is, already the case. My deep love of music became much simpler—music became a means to express that native Happiness. I found that in this freedom I started to really get into music. It was an ordinary occupation, but a happy one. Why not?

This has been a great lesson, but it is really very simple. As Da Love-Ananda used to shout at me when I would play the cello for him, "Byron—play from the point of view of God!"

CHAPTER TEN

The Transmission of Happiness

The Invisible Spirit

Even though the air around us is full of radio and television signals of all kinds, they are essentially unnoticed by our bodily senses. The story is told that a man once had a tooth filled by his dentist and discovered that he was somehow tuned in to the local radio station. Imagine meeting this man! What if he began tapping his foot to some hidden melody, exclaiming "What a great song!" If he didn't explain himself, we would probably think he was crazy. Should he try to help us "tune in" by describing the song, even singing a bit of it, we wouldn't hear it, even though the music courses through the airwaves all around us.

Likewise, the very space around us and even our body-minds themselves are pervaded by a mysterious Feeling or Force, which in the Way of the Heart is called "Spirit", though it has been known by many names, such as the "Current of Life", "Kundalini", and the "Goddess". Everyone can intuit this Feeling, or Spirit—which is Love. It is the radiant energy that fills our beings when we are completely, thoughtlessly, unreasonably Happy and that communicates itself to others contagiously, beyond any words or gestures. The Spirit is not only the Happiness that is communicated, but it is the medium of communication as well. It pervades all beings and things, interconnecting everyone and everything in a great Web of Life.

Ordinarily, however, we don't tangibly Commune with and receive the Spirit, or regularly feel it as an active Force and source of transformation throughout our daily life. Consequently, simply to hear from someone that this Spirit does exist is not enough to bring about immersion or "Baptism" in the Spirit beyond all doubting and thinking. Even the most complete description of how the Spirit feels is still only a description. So the traditional spiritual admonitions to Commune with the Spirit or to surrender in the Spirit are not particularly useful for us by themselves.

It is not that we are missing some mechanism, like a dental filling, that would enable us to tune in to the Divine Spirit or the Feeling of Being. The ability to Commune with the All-Pervading Divine Spirit exists in all of us. But most of the time that ability is only potential, not actual. Just as it never occurs to us to try to listen to the local broadcast without a radio, we are generally not aware that Communion with the Spirit is possible. And were we to become convinced of the possibility of such attunement, most of us would not have the slightest idea of how to go about it.

The psychic or higher mental aspects of ourselves that we do not use, or that fall into disuse, do not develop to full capacity. People who have had a leg or an arm in a cast for a long time know this, because generally they need to develop their muscular strength again, or even relearn how to use the limb, once the cast is removed. Of course they have the advantage of having already learned to use a leg or an arm. But the process of awakening to spiritual Communion is more like learning to use an organ that most of us don't even know we have. In fact, Heart-Master Da Love-Ananda describes spiritual practice as an utterly revolutionary change that is equivalent to growing new legs and arms.

DA LOVE-ANANDA: What must take place, if spiritual life is to be true, is not just a change in your mind, an inner awakening, a good feeling about everything. Spiritual processes do not occur in the subjective nonsense that people associate with religion—all this vicarious belief and vicarious salvation—as if real Awakening were just a matter of asking some silly questions or going to a few lectures for the weekend! That is not Enlightenment. Enlightenment is a literal change of the whole body. When you have acquired the human form, the literal change that must occur in the body is not really so much in its outward appearance, because you already have the necessary structure. But the changes that must occur are literal, psycho-physical changes, just as literal as if you were to acquire more legs and arms, except that the most dramatic changes occur in dimensions different from the outward shape of the body. The change is as literal as evolving from a dinosaur to a human being, and it is as dramatic as that, but it principally occurs at more subtle levels of the physics of the bodily being. There are literal changes in the nervous system, literal changes in the chemistry of the body, literal changes in the structural functioning of the brain.

You cannot realize such change in a weekend. [1]

How do we realize Enlightenment, complete Happiness, or unconditional Love, even if we are willing to commit our entire lives to realizing it? We may intuit the Spirit, but we are unable to hold on to that intuition, however attracted we seem to be. Ordinarily we are so absorbed in day-to-day affairs that our attention is overwhelmingly bound to mundane levels of experiencing. Our common awareness simply does not include the dimension of the Spirit.

This is why the appearance of the Enlightened Adept, or Heart-Master, is traditionally so highly valued. The Heart-Master magnifies the Spirit through forms we can easily relate to—forms we can see and hear and touch—his human body-mind, his written communication, even the places where he has lived or put his special attention.

Heart-Master Da Love-Ananda appears in modern times, functioning as a ''Transmitter'' or an ''Agent'' of the Spirit. He describes the extraordinary process of spiritual Transmission that takes place in relationship to the Heart-Master:

DA LOVE-ANANDA: The gross aspects of ourselves function very much like transmitter-receivers. This gross body is a living bio-form. It has the capacity to operate in a field of energy, to transfer energies, and to be in sympathy, therefore, with fields of energy beyond the physical body.

A person who is balanced and in good condition can transfer energy to another for healing purposes. He or she may perhaps even use a thought intention to project the healing energy, but such energy basically works within a shorter range. Healing is possible at a longer range, but in that case it uses a different tuning-in mechanism.

The process that underlies my relationship to people operates within these fields of energy. It makes use, in other words, of the subtler physics of the cosmos. For people to make use of my Company, they must have developed sufficient self-understanding, or at least freedom in themselves, that they can participate with me at a subtler physical level, or at a level that corresponds to the subtler physics of the cosmos.

Just as people turn on a TV set and tune in to a particular station, devotees can use their whole life of practice and association with me to tune up their own mechanism in order to tune in to my Field. Practitioners of this Way perform pujas [ceremonies of ritual worship] and other means to accomplish this tuning-in process, but they should understand the underlying mechanism. It does not exist in the realm of fancy. It is a real process. It is simply operative at a different level of the physics of reality. You can discover for yourself that there actually is this subtler realm, this complex system of light-radiation wherein we exist, by freeing up energy and attention through the process of your practice and beginning to fall sympathetically into the complete Realm wherein we exist.

At present, it is as if we are in a great room full of television sets and none of us believes in TV, or has ever watched it. It is as if none of us have even seen TV. All these sets are just sitting around here, but nobody is turning them on and tuning in. That is how we live. We have all these appliances here, and yet everybody stands around saying, "Is there a God?" "Is there anything greater than this?" Every now and then somebody goes over, plugs in the set, and turns it on, and everybody marvels. Usually, though, people only relate to that gesture in a silly and fascinated manner.

The Adept is somebody who turns on the set and shows you its full potential. He himself becomes a Transmitter and a great Station and helps you tune in to him and create a new Way of life. That is the point. The process with which you become involved through all that is a process of growth through tuning in to the full Dimensional Existence that is our Life, our Being.[2]

Attraction

When you were a young boy (or girl) you probably wanted very little to do with children of the opposite sex. Perhaps one day you noticed that a great change had come over you (and them). Suddenly, one special girl (or boy) was attractive—really attractive! You began to do all kinds of things you would never have done before. You didn't need to pretend or believe anything in order to make this change. It was the natural outcome of your attraction to the opposite sex.

Similarly, many devotees have said that when they began to study Da Love-Ananda's Wisdom-Teaching they were cautious and unclear about entering into a spiritual relationship with the Heart-Master himself. And that is fine—it is no more appropriate or necessary for students to feel they must struggle with a spiritual relationship to Heart-Master Da Love-Ananda than for an elementary school student to feel pressured to grapple with romance.

The spiritual relationship to the Heart-Master is a natural outcome of listening and pondering. When the Teaching Argument has begun to make its point in life, you naturally begin to awaken to the Heart-Master's true Nature, which is the same as your own true Nature. Then Heart-Master Da Love-Ananda becomes more and more Attractive. You become sensitive to the Heart-Master's Transmission of Happiness, or Spirit-Baptism.

DA LOVE-ANANDA: The essence of the Way of the Heart is the Transmission of Spirit. This Transmission Intoxicates you, but if you have not understood yourself, you cannot use my Spirit-Blessing. You will shut it down. Therefore, you are only prepared to practice in Truth when you have used my Teaching to the point of understanding. Then you will receive my Baptism and you will practice Communion with this Transmitted Sublimity from moment to moment. That is the Way. Then you will change your entire life, but not until then.

Therefore, you must prepare yourself to use my Transmission by using my Argument—not just by listening to it, but by combining yourself with it—to understand the knot of self-contraction, how it works as a mechanism that shuts down the Beauty of Infinite Life. When you have understood me to that degree, then you can receive my Baptism truly and begin to practice.

To practice is to submit yourself to the Energy of the Spirit, to life in the Spirit, to my Baptism. When you have contacted the Spirit most profoundly, then you can live your whole life with the Spirit and give yourself up to It altogether. The Spirit sublimes the being. It makes a wonder out of existence, It lifts you out of the subhuman round of un-Happiness. It awakens your emotion. It awakens your faith. Therefore, until you have tasted my Baptism, you do not know what I am talking about, because I talk the Spirit only to prepare you to taste It. And when you have heard me, then you can suck It up, luxuriate in It, and fall into It.

Spiritual life is Intoxication. You must become Intoxicated in the Spirit.

I come here to give you everything without the slightest reluctance. I am not here to tell you about some dreadful ego. I am here to Wonder and Marvel with you about the Great One.[3]

Da Love-Ananda calls the awakening to his Transmission of Intoxicating Happiness "seeing". Seeing is reception of the Heart-Master's spiritual Blessing to the degree that life in the Spirit becomes possible. Seeing is love. It is the conversion of the heart from self-contraction to self-transcending surrender to the Divine Spirit-Force. It is the awakening of devotion, the reorientation of the personality to the spiritual Presence that melts the heart and purifies body and mind. To see is to know that your life is carried by the Current of Happiness.

The Conscious Process

But seeing, or reception of the Spirit-Blessing, is not a passive process. It must be actively, consciously engaged:

DA LOVE-ANANDA: If you are not presently locating this Current, then you are unconsciously and literally forgetting It, contracting from It. You must consciously associate attention with this spiritual Current, or Blissful Being, or you will unconsciously withdraw from It.

This is why I call meditation the "conscious process".[4]

Being extends even beyond the dimension of Spirit into the dimension of Consciousness. And Consciousness is the primary Principle of existence:

DA LOVE-ANANDA: Consciousness is not in the body.
Consciousness is not identical to the brain or the
nervous system. Consciousness is an utterly Free
Location or Disposition of Being. It seems to be
associated and bound up with the body-mind, and
therefore we tend to become full of ideas that are
expressions of doubt. We tend to wonder, "Well,
perhaps this Consciousness is just a secondary result
of some kind of molecular activity in the nervous
system. It's really brain-based. It's just naive to think
that Consciousness is some kind of immortal principle." From our conventional position that kind of
thinking could be true, but to dwell upon it is merely
to magnify our doubt. What we must do is investigate
Consciousness and see how Consciousness is related
to all the other kinds of phenomena.

If we do that, we find that Consciousness is
related in precisely the same way to the stomach as it
is to the brain, to the bird in the yard as it is to the
hair on the head, to the eye as it is to the toes, to the
outer form of the body as it is to the inner. It is
related equally or in the same manner to all of these.
It is unique even in the context of psycho-physical
existence. It is obviously the primary Principle, not
some secondary effect, of our real, pscho-physical
existence. It is the reason for that existence, the
import of it, the significance of it.[5]

Because Consciousness is the fundamental principle, the
conscious process is the primary practice of the Way of the
Heart:

DA LOVE-ANANDA: The fundamental context of this Way
in any of its stages is the moment to moment practice
of understanding or insight, which is the fundamental form of this Way and which is realized as true
meditation or what I call the conscious process—the
present exercise of insight or intuitive intelligence.
The fundamental exercise of this Way is not any

other method that is at best, if at all, a consequence of understanding, a technique that could be practiced without understanding. The practice of understanding is not a Godless exercise. It is worship of God in Spirit and in Truth.[6]

And again:

DA LOVE-ANANDA: The conscious process is the epitome of the Way. It is the essence and ultimate, most fundamental exercise of the Way, but it is necessarily associated with the total culture of life. The reason for this is that the ego, the self-contraction, the character that is Narcissus, is not merely some superficial notion. My conception of Narcissus applies to every single aspect, every part, function, state, relation, and condition of the self. There is no part of the manifest self that is not characterized by this character of Narcissus, the self-contraction, the complex avoidance of relationship. It is not merely a superficial part of you, underneath which there is this eternally free essence with which you should identify. Even that essence underneath it all, that fundamental sense of self-consciousness, is a fraction of this total character that is Narcissus. This total character must be understood and transcended in every feature, in every function, in every part, in every relation, in every state—waking, dreaming, and sleeping.[7]

CHAPTER ELEVEN

The First Glance

by Ty Koontz

Although I had been studying Da Love-Ananda's Wisdom-Teaching daily for about two years, I had only been formally associated with The Free Daist Communion for about two months when I was invited to attend a celebration at The Mountain of Attention Sanctuary in September 1979. As an utter newcomer I had no expectations that I would see Da Love-Ananda.

When I heard that, in a typically unpredictable and compassionate gesture, Da Love-Ananda had decided to attend the formal occasion with everyone who came to the celebration, I was overjoyed. But because of my previous association with a different teacher, I had an unconscious assumption about the upcoming event. I thought I had experienced spiritual Transmission before, and I assumed I knew what was in store for me.

Soon I saw the crowd begin to stir, and I knew that Da Love-Ananda had to be somewhere in sight. But the only person I could see approaching was a wrinkled old man with long, white hair and a full, bushy grey beard. He was wearing an unusual white outfit with a distinctive hat. With a start, I recognized Da Love-Ananda among the wrinkles. As I bowed, I was in a state of shock and confusion. What could have happened to age him so?

When I sat up again, there was Da Love-Ananda in the same striking outfit. But he was young, brown-haired, and clean-shaven! All my preconceptions fled. I no longer had any idea what I was in for.

Then Da Love-Ananda looked at me.

In a split second my entire field of vision became almost white with brilliant light. Da Love-Ananda's eyes were infinite pools of intensity. A fire burned in my spine, setting my entire nervous system ablaze. I began to feel overwhelmed with a glorious, mind-dissolving, unnamable emotion. The intensity of light and emotion rose higher, and still higher. I had the clear intuition that the spiritual Power flowing through Da Love-Ananda would carry me as far and as fast as I was willing to allow. My deepest desires for spiritual revelation were being fulfilled, and at the same time all the habits and attachments that would hold me in place were being consumed by the fire of Da Love-Ananda's spiritual Transmission. Suddenly, I felt myself drawn outside the limits of my body, and I became afraid.

Da Love-Ananda looked away and the experience ceased abruptly. There were no aftereffects of my fear—no pounding heart, no heaving breath, no stressful chemistry. There was only my astonishment at the powerful process that had just taken place and disappointment in my ability to respond fully: I had been offered everything that my heart cried out for, but like the man who brought a teacup to the ocean I had been able to receive only the tiniest fraction of what was freely given. It was obvious to me that I had stopped the process short of its fulfillment. The rest of the occasion was a further lesson in self-knowledge, revealing the mechanisms by which I defend myself against the Infinite. I understood completely why the right use of Da Love-Ananda's spiritual Company requires real preparation. As he once put it:

> Devotees are required to live in the fire and be purified. And only when you have been in the fire long enough does it begin to enlighten you. When you have burned up in it, then it is Light. Until that time it is heat.
>
> Thus, if I sit with you, if I look at you, a fire is given to you. It is also the Enlightening Radiance, but

its fundamental effect is fiery for a time. Therefore,
do not look for casual contact with me. [1]

So much for my first occasion with the Heart-Master, I
thought.

But Da Love-Ananda had initiated a process in me that
continues even today. In the days that followed, every time I
remembered him a huge wave of love would swell unbidden
in my heart, and I would feel unreasonably Happy. A few days
after the event during the long drive back to my home, I
experienced a further revelation of Da Love-Ananda's powerful
Transmission. At a rest stop on the freeway I found myself
passing judgment on a stranger, mentally writing him off as
the kind of person I dislike on sight. Almost unwillingly, I saw
my unlove over against my relationship to Da Love-Ananda,
and I was startled to feel the pain of my self-righteous judgment of this man. But when I remembered Da Love-Ananda, to
my astonishment I discovered that I was in love not only with
him but with the stranger I had so casually dismissed a
moment ago. This was so unexpected that I became disoriented. By what miracle was I able to feel love for someone
who an instant before I had seen as my opponent?

As I waited for my wife to return to the car, I noticed how
beautiful the rest area was with its fine shade trees. By the
time we drove off I was beaming with Happiness. My wife
began to read to me from one of Da Love-Ananda's books as
we drove along. The scenery appeared more and more beautiful, even somehow more three-dimensional. A great joy
expanded throughout my being. Da Love-Ananda's words
seemed especially true to me, an exquisite expression of his
Realization. Something remarkable was happening to me. I
had no idea where it would lead, but I felt I was in the midst
of a mysterious process that was directly and obviously con-
nected with my relationship to Heart-Master Da Love-Ananda. I
began to cooperate with the process, feeling my heart connection to Da Love-Ananda and allowing events to unfold as they
would.

Then, at some undefined point, I became aware that the
words my wife was reading to me were not philosophical or

abstract. Da Love-Ananda was simply describing what was obvious to him and what was now obvious to me, through his Agency. I and the whole world were unmistakably afloat in a single Consciousness and that Consciousness was Love. Nothing had changed. Busy thoughts of all kinds, positive and negative, still passed through my mind, but they were like splinters floating on the ocean of Consciousness. They had no power to disturb my enjoyment of and inherence in this Love. I was still driving. Traffic and scenery were sailing by. But it was all Love. The trucks zooming by were Love, and so were the truck drivers. I was Love. My wife was Love. The trees, the road, the posts, and the signs were all happily, wonderfully, absurdly alive with Love, animated by Love alone.

It was completely apparent to me that there is only One Being. I could see how we view people and objects as separate, discrete "things", but that was just a superficial imposition on the One Reality that was utterly, naturally obvious to me. It was all absurdly humorous, and even a little crazy. But there was only unreasonable, unattainable, undeserved Happiness and Love. Nothing else was possible.

What is more, I recognized the One Being to be the same One I had felt overwhelming my body-mind some days earlier when Da Love-Ananda had glanced in my direction. Only this time, through Grace, I had been absorbed in that One beyond all fear and separation.

After some hours, that graceful understanding faded, but my gratitude for Da Love-Ananda's Wisdom-Teaching and spiritual Blessing has continued to grow and deepen. Many times since then Da Love-Ananda has Blessed me with the gift of that understanding. Countless times each day I see my self-possession over against Da Love-Ananda's spiritual Presence, even though he is thousands of miles away, and I see once again how I am creating my own unhappiness. The Way is often difficult, and the vision of the "knot" of the self is not pleasant. But I have seen that without self-understanding any moment of happiness is only partial and fleeting. And Da Love-Ananda's compassionate Heart-Transmission shines beyond the limitations of self. His Transmission is always available, drawing his devotees to the Happiness that he is.

SECTION FOUR

THE CULTURE OF PRACTICE

Until we have created a human order that is fundamentally free of mutual threat, it will not be common for people to live in a truly awakened and peaceful state, not only of mind, but of body (or the total body-mind). The body-mind must receive the signals that the stressful world has been overcome, that we need not fear, that we presently have a peaceful human society, not a society full of bombs and benighted craziness. To create a human sanctuary for higher adaptation and the ultimate transcendence of Man is a true urge, even the primal human urge.

Da Love-Ananda
Scientific Proof of the Existence
of God Will Soon Be Announced
by the White House! *pp. 239–41*

1986

CHAPTER TWELVE

The Principle of Retreat

Traditionally, when an individual wished to intensify the practice of spiritual life, he or she went on retreat, renouncing for a time the activities and habits that might draw energy and attention away from the spiritual process. Living in a quiet and secluded environment and embracing a simplified way of life, the individual concentrated all his or her energy and attention on spiritual practice. This "Principle of Retreat" is also the foundation of practice in the Way of the Heart.

The Principle of Retreat comprises two disciplines: the supportive "discipline of the body-mind", or "equanimity", and the primary "discipline of attention", or "understanding". The Principle of Retreat is engaged even when you first study the Teaching Argument or attend a public presentation. At an introductory lecture, for instance, you practice the discipline of the body-mind through your bodily participation in the event, as you remain seated in one place for an hour or two. And you practice the discipline of attention by giving your attention or listening to the presentation. You forgo other possible distractions and attractions and devote yourself, body and mind, to pondering the Teaching Argument.

The Discipline of the Body-Mind

The supportive discipline of the body-mind is simple, sane, and ordinary, although to make right use of the practical disciplines requires a degree of real self-understanding. These disciplines not only balance and rejuvenate the body-mind, but they also frustrate the separative habits of Narcissus. Beginning practitioners observe their tendencies toward consolation and self-indulgence on the one hand and toward states of low energy and life-denying withholding on the other, all the habits with which they have become comfortable over a lifetime of separation and seeking.

The practice of spiritual life is a difficult ordeal, but not because Da Love-Ananda has made it so, or because the practices are technically difficult. The true spiritual ordeal has always been difficult. It involves a profound transformation, a turnabout at every level of the being. It requires you to break all your old, deep-set habits and to grow beyond yourself continually. To begin to live on a different basis causes friction, or "heat"—the fire of frustrating the tendencies that reinforce our unhappiness. We are addicted to the programs of Narcissus, and to overcome this addiction requires a great struggle.

The heat created by self-surrender through discipline releases new energy that is no longer bound to the habits of Narcissus. It is conscious energy, not energy sleeping comfortably in a well-worn groove. This heightened level of free energy is, especially at first, difficult to handle. It is a little bit like trying to carry a steaming, brim-full bowl of soup without spilling it on your hands. It requires you to be awake. This heat is valuable for spiritual practice, although it may not always feel good. But more and more over time this heat is transformed into the fire of attraction to the Divine, and ultimately, the discipline of the body-mind is fulfilled in God-Realization, or utter, continuous, and eternal Freedom from identification with bodily and mental limits.

The Discipline of Attention

The discipline of attention, the primary discipline of the Principle of Retreat, first develops, through study, into pondering of the Teaching Argument in daily life. As your

practice of the Way strengthens, pondering naturally and pro-
gressively evolves into the capacity for real meditation. And
meditation is ultimately fulfilled in the transcendence of attention altogether in God-Realization.

During the period of "listening" you come to see and
understand the unhappiness that drives your search. The
motive to self-transcendence awakens and in time it becomes
your primary impulse. More and more, you uncover the hidden workings of Narcissus, the self-contraction, in the ordinary
events of your daily life, and you come to understand the
unique way that you personally live out the drama of the ego,
or the life of Narcissus. In this manner, real self-understanding
awakens, and you begin to intuit the Divine Condition or
Reality. And through attraction to the Divine Condition, you
fall out of sympathy with the action that is Narcissus.

Now impelled by the awakened impulse to Liberation,
you enter the stage of "seeing", or the conversion of the heart
from self-attention to God-Communion through attraction to
the all-pervading Spirit. In this stage, which takes place within
a complete spiritual culture, you contact the Radiance of the
Divine Condition in meditation and from moment to moment
in daily life. As your reception of the Spirit becomes steady,
your functional life is purified and harmonized in all areas—
physical, emotional, and mental. Then you are drawn by Grace
through the various subtle dimensions of mysticism and yoga,
which spiritualize the being.

Many extraordinary experiences, including states of temporary absorption in bliss, may occur during this spiritualizing
stage of practice. But in the Way of the Heart experiences in
themselves are never the point. Ultimately, every experience,
even the most sublime experiences of mystical and transcendental Bliss, must be transcended in the intuition of unconditional Happiness.

As Da Love-Ananda has Revealed, practice of the Way of
the Heart inevitably leads to the Realization of Consciousness
Itself ("Sahaj Samadhi"), or the Realization of Identity with
the Divine Person and Reality, beyond all experience of body,
mind, and world. Finally, the God-Realized Devotee is Trans-
lated into the Divine Domain eternally beyond all knowing.

Da Love-Ananda has described this ultimate Process of Translation or Outshining:

> DA LOVE-ANANDA: If you enter into that Consciousness, that Realization, most profoundly, acknowledging It, It is Being Itself, uncreated. It is not the result of anything. It is Bliss Inherently. It is Happiness. It is Delight, apparently played upon but never fundamentally changing. If you are perfectly established in That Which is always already the case before the self-contraction changes your view, there is nothing but Self-Existing Consciousness, Inherently Blissful and Free, requiring absolutely nothing. You simply Stand as That recognizing what arises. Eventually all this arising is Outshined.
>
> If you shine a light into a dark room, at first it will fall on the objects. If you intensify that light to the absolute degree, it would become something like an atomic explosion. The light would become so profound that it would shine through everything. Everything would become transparent in it. Everything would become white hot in it. There would be no distinctions. So it is with the Self, recognizing what arises. What arises may appear at first to be something like objects illumined in Consciousness. Eventually they cease to be discerned or noticed. There is no body-mind or world, no objects or relations. In the Realization of Consciousness there are no such things anyway. They are nothing but modifications of Consciousness. They have no independent existence. But in the Perfection of this Realization in Translation no conditions are discerned. It is not a matter of ascent, then, or descent or here or there. It is just the Divine Condition Itself Outshining all possibilities, all contraction, all tendency to modify. [1]

The Basis of the Way

For those who have practiced to the point of true "hearing" and clear "seeing", the basis of this great process is the initiatory Transmission of Happiness granted by the God-Realized Heart-Master. Through spiritual initiation (generally received via Heart-Master Da Love-Ananda's Empowered Agencies), the devotee learns to contact the Divine Condition from moment to moment. Therefore, the Heart-Master's Transmission (or Transmitted Presence) is the Means for the devotee's ultimate Awakening.

For the practicing devotee, both disciplines of the Principle of Retreat are founded in the spiritual relationship to the Heart-Master. Without Da Love-Ananda's transforming Influence, all "disciplines" recommended in the Way of the Heart are no more than empty ritual and all "understanding" is an illusion of the body-mind. But when they are practiced in right devotional (or spiritual) relationship to the Heart-Master, the disciplines of the body-mind and attention become effective means of submission to Mastery by the graceful Accomplishing Power of the Divine.

At this stage of his Blessing Work, Heart-Master Da Love-Ananda generally Transmits his Blessing through the Agency of the existing community of his practicing devotees (and through the Agency of retreat Sanctuaries he has Empowered for the use of his devotees). This initiation takes place not through any individuals who might function as independent "gurus" but rather through the community as a whole, without any self-conscious intention on the part of its members or its cultural leaders. When the community gathers in meditative and devotional occasions, Heart-Master Da Love-Ananda's Transmission is spontaneously magnified for the sake of all.

Da Love-Ananda will likely continue to remain personally available to mature devotees (in the advanced practicing stages of the Way) who engage in meditation retreats at the Translation Island Hermitage Sanctuary. Likewise, it remains possible that he may occasionally accept invitations (extended by the general community of practitioners) to travel to other Sanctuaries and retreat centers, and thus to continue his

Blessing Work while in residence (and in the care of practicing devotees) around the world.

The Free Daist Communion

The Free Daist Communion has the responsibility to communicate and provide the cultural context for the study and practice of the Way that Heart-Master Da Love-Ananda has Revealed. The primary purpose of The Free Daist Communion, a tax-exempt, non-profit religious organization, is to serve Heart-Master Da Love-Ananda's Work to Awaken individuals directly to the Living Divine Reality. The Communion exists to fulfill four great obligations: (1) to care for (and otherwise to provide for appropriate access to) the sacred treasures, or the Heart-Master and the principal means of his Agency, namely, the sacred Wisdom-Teaching and the Empowered Sanctuaries; (2) to disseminate the Wisdom-Teaching of Heart-Master Da Love-Ananda; (3) to provide educational and cultural services for its members and the general public; and (4) to give voice in the general public to the Wisdom that counters and balances the modern trends of scientific materialism and religious provincialism.

The Services of The Free Daist Communion

The Free Daist Communion is the general or inclusive name of the total institutional body of men and women who freely choose to study, practice, and fulfill the Great Way of the Heart Revealed by Da Love-Ananda. There are seven stages of practice in The Free Daist Communion.

The first stage of practice develops in The Laughing Man Institute, which educates the general public, Friends, students, and beginning practitioners. The Laughing Man Institute provides presentations, lectures, seminars, courses, and other cultural opportunities to serve the serious understanding (and application) of Da Love-Ananda's Liberating Teaching Arguments and the practice of the Way that he has Revealed.

As of this writing, The Laughing Man Institute has thirteen public Centers around the world. In North America: northern California (San Rafael), southern California (Santa Monica), Seattle, Chicago, Austin, Baltimore, Boston, and Toronto. In Europe: London and Amsterdam. In Australia: Melbourne and Sydney. In New Zealand: Auckland.

Practicing stages two through seven are divided into four cultural organizations, or Fellowships:

Practicing stages two and three are developed and completed within The Dawn Horse Fellowship, stages four and five within The Ajna Dharma Fellowship, and stage six within The Advaitayana Buddhist Fellowship. The seventh or the Enlightened stage of practice is demonstrated within The Crazy Wisdom Fellowship.

All of the instructions, initiations, tests, and signs of maturity and Realization at each stage of practice have been summarized and described in great detail in the published Teaching of Heart-Master Da Love-Ananda.

CHAPTER THIRTEEN

The Community of the Heart

The Spiritual Practice of Community

Once a devotee was exclaiming how strongly he had felt Da Love-Ananda's Presence, far from the Adept's physical Company and in a place that Da Love-Ananda had never visited. Da Love-Ananda interrupted him to explain that he has a constant Transcendental and psychic association with the place and that he has also Empowered certain sacred articles to be found there. "But," he continued, "I am also there because you are there! I have personally Blessed you, and when you and others remember me, then I am Present."

Wherever new centers have opened—in North America, Europe, Australia, and New Zealand—the story is the same. Any time community members yield their combined attention to the Transmission of Happiness contacted through Da Love-Ananda and his Agencies, all are enveloped and transformed by the power of this Communion. Unquestionably such gatherings magnify the spiritual Blessing that can always be contacted in Da Love-Ananda's spiritual Company.

Unlike conventional gatherings, which are generally organized for the sake of secular purposes, the community of devotees is a devotional culture. For this reason community life is only fully embraced when the devotional response begins to awaken in the devotee. In the stages of pondering the Wisdom-Teaching and preparing to take up the Way of the

Heart, full participation in spiritual community is neither necessary nor even possible, although everyone is invited to enjoy the benefits of community involvement by attending presentations and classes on the Wisdom-Teaching.

The sacred discipline of community is a mature spiritual practice involving the mutual reception of and response to Da Love-Ananda's Transmission of Blessing. It is through the heart, or the emotional dimension, that devotees receive the spiritual Blessing that ever flows from Da Love-Ananda. And that devotional response is particularly served by occasions of group meditation, ceremonial worship, devotional singing, and other devotional activities, since they awaken the emotions and open the hearts of devotees. When devotees gather in Communion, these gatherings are a channel for the Transforming Power of the Divine.

The intensity generated by such events is often wondrous. The opening ceremony for a weekend celebration at The Mountain of Attention Sanctuary in mid-September 1984 was just such a gathering. Because many people drove long distances to reach the Sanctuary, the occasion was well under way when people from outlying areas began to arrive. Already, the radiant Energy of Divine Blessing was pouring out from the open-air temple where the event was being held. Devotees' reception of Da Love-Ananda's Transmission of Happiness had magnified that Transmission to all attending the event. The Adept's Divine Blessing was carried especially on the sound of the chanting, which could be heard even at the gates of the Sanctuary.

As the Sanctuary gatekeeper relates, "People arrived tired and road-weary, but as they reached the gate and heard the chanting, the force of Blessing revitalized them and awakened their hearts. The impact was obvious. Their faces brightened with recognition of the Presence. Though Da Love-Ananda was physically over five thousand miles away, they knew they were entering his spiritual Domain. The Transmission was so strong that the hairs on my head were standing on end."

Such events are frequent occurrences among the community of devotees, an ongoing demonstration of why a major portion of Da Love-Ananda's Work has been the development and stabilization of a sacred community. As devotees make use of his Wisdom-Teaching and the other Empowered Agencies as well as occasions in his spiritual Company, they mature in spiritual practice, and his vision of community will manifest more and more over time in centers throughout the world. He fully intends the community as a whole, rather than any individual, to act as his successor. Only the God-Realized Adept is qualified to exercise the role of Heart-Master, but the culture of practitioners, once it has achieved maturity, will become more and more transparent to his Transmission of Happiness and thus provide a vehicle of Agency that is eminently full and instructive.

Already the community serves as Da Love-Ananda's Agency in significant ways, though not through any self-conscious manipulation of energies nor any strategic intentions to bring about changes. The function of Agency arises spontaneously in devotees and in the community as a whole, often without their knowledge, and simply by virtue of their reception of Da Love-Ananda's Transmission of Happiness.

DA LOVE-ANANDA: The Community is in itself a form of meditation, a form of devotion. Therefore, when devotees get together they tend to turn one another quite naturally to the Guru, to Satsang [literally, the "Company of Truth"]. Individually, they tend to become associated with their dramas, their changes, their limitations. But as soon as they enter into one another's company, it is as if they were reminding one another of Satsang, even though they might not outwardly be saying it. That reminder in itself is meditation, so you naturally feel it more strongly at those times of gathering. Also, you are entering into the company of many others in whom this Siddhi [transforming power] is active, perhaps in different ways than it is in your own case. Limitations that may be yours may not be active in some of the others, so you feel the Force of the Siddhi more purely represented to you at those times, because your own limitations are transcended by the Force as it freely appears in others. Just so, there may be areas in yourself that are not obstructed, but which are obstructed in others, and those others feel the Power of Satsang more intensely because of your presence, or the presence of several like you.[1]

This is the secret of spiritual community: our mutual Communion with the Living Divine Reality. When we gather together in the mood of self-transcendence and jointly yield our lives to the Divine Condition, the effects can be even more potent than those realized by individual surrender. Even the tests and demands of community life produce self-understanding. Seen in the light of community, Narcissus can no longer be coddled or ignored—he must be transcended.

On one of many such occasions Da Love-Ananda once invited the entire community, then numbering about three hundred members, to sit with him in Western Face Cathedral at The Mountain of Attention. Bringing gifts of fruit or flowers, people entered the Cathedral and were seated in rows, entirely filling the meditation hall. After Da Love-Ananda had taken his seat at the front of the hall but before meditation began, the community sang a slow and melodious chant while devotees approached Da Love-Ananda's chair to offer their gifts.

To make such an intimate gesture to the Heart-Master is a real opportunity for quickening one's spiritual practice. "As I approached the dais," one man recalls, "my attention was riveted to Da Love-Ananda, and my body-mind was open to his Transmission. I could feel his Presence intensely, and when I offered my gift, I was overwhelmed by the intimacy of the occasion and Da Love-Ananda's powerful Blessing. As I turned to go back to my seat, I looked out over the community, whose faces and hearts were turned as one to the Heart-Master while they sang in a single, strong voice. I was again overwhelmed by Da Love-Ananda's powerful Presence, communicated to me through the Agency of the community. The community was Da Love-Ananda's mirror image."

When a practitioner simply surrenders his or her attention to the Divine through devotion to the God-Realized Adept, the Divine Transmission spontaneously begins its Work, purifying and Awakening the devotee. Only in that surrendered state does the devotee become a spontaneous channel or Agency for others.

A woman recalls that one day, as she was leaving Great Food Dish, the dining room at The Mountain of Attention Sanctuary, she saw devotees nearby with their hands raised in a devotional gesture. She knew Da Love-Ananda must be passing and she quickly stepped onto the porch to enjoy the sight of the Master. But he had just walked out of sight. Disappointed, she turned back toward Great Food Dish, still full of longing to see the Heart-Master.

> As I turned, I saw another devotee facing the
> place where the Heart-Master had been, his hands

still raised in acknowledgement and surrender. The look on his face was bright with happiness and devotion. He was obviously transfigured in Communion with Da Love-Ananda. It was as if he were a transparent vehicle for Da Love-Ananda's Blessing, so potently was the Master's Presence communicated to me as I regarded his radiant face. I was unable to look away. This incident greatly impressed me with the form of Agency that the community can be, and that Da Love-Ananda intends it to be.

Perfection Is Not the Point

The devotional relationship to the God-Realized Adept is the essence of spiritual life. But inevitably your character weaknesses will trip you up and interfere with the relationship. When that happens, the value of community becomes truly apparent. Although your "problems" may seem to you to be simply the way things are, another person whose spiritual practice is untroubled in that area may reveal the situation in a truer light.

One woman, upon first hearing about Da Love-Ananda from a friend, spontaneously experienced his Transmission of Spirit-Blessing. However, when she inquired about taking up spiritual practice in the community, she was dismayed to learn of the disciplines that would eventually be her responsibility. Though she had wished to pursue her newfound relationship to Da Love-Ananda, she felt she could not face the inevitability of assuming the disciplines.

Some time later, the woman was invited to a dinner and presentation on the Way of the Heart. She was given her plate, filled generously with a mouth-watering vegetarian feast, and was seated next to another woman. Just as she was about to enjoy her meal, she noticed the plate next to hers. It so happened that the mature practitioner beside her had temporarily adopted a relatively simple diet—on her plate was a plain baked potato and a small undressed salad.

Immediately, the woman began to feel embarrassed and guilty. "How can I eat this sumptuous meal," she thought,

"when the woman beside me must suffer such an unappetiz-
ing diet? How cruel for her to be seated by me!" But as she
watched the devotee eat and talk, she observed that the
devotee said not a word of complaint about her meal. Instead,
smiling and relaxed, she spoke with obvious feeling of her
relationship to Da Love-Ananda and how happy she was to
notice that relationship strengthening as her discipline freed
energy and attention for spiritual practice.

The woman, feeling her own state of present unhappiness
despite the delicious meal before her, realized that her com-
panion was blessed. The devotee was so attracted by Da Love-
Ananda's spiritual offering that her attention was naturally
drawn to the Happiness of that spiritual relationship rather
than the seeming austerity of the disciplines she had temporarily adopted. Her living demonstration of the usefulness
of discipline allowed the woman to feel the attractiveness of
spiritual life. And every devotee can attest to many times when
some aspect of the Way seemed troublesome or unclear until
they observed its demonstration in members of the
community.

Our community is still developing, but it will never be a
perfectly ordered gathering of perpetually smiling, saintly, and
faultless individuals. It will always be composed of individuals
in all stages of practice, who embody all kinds of human
qualities, some admirable and some reflecting immaturity. Da
Love-Ananda once cautioned:

> DA LOVE-ANANDA: There is no point in becoming "con-
> cerned" about the Community. The sadhana [spiri-
> tual practice] of the Community is no more a matter
> of concern for what appears than your personal
> sadhana is a matter of concern for the qualities that
> arise in meditation. The Community can only be-
> come schizophrenic, righteous, self-conscious, and
> peculiar by thinking that the realization of the Com-
> munity, as I have described it, is identical to a certain
> exterior manifestation that is perfect, noncultic, bril-
> liant, and all of the rest. Then the Community will
> always be looking at itself to make sure its ass is not

hanging out. All of that is itself cultic concern. As long as human individuals are the substance of the Community (and that is forever!), the tendency will be present in each person every hour of every day to manifest the conditions and dramas of Narcissus.[2]

And again:

DA LOVE-ANANDA: The Community is not to be goal-oriented toward any kind of perfection. Sadhana is not a matter of accumulation and attainment, whether it is done in the form of the Community or in the form of any individual. Sadhana is a matter of undoing, dissolution, understanding, not accumulation, not attainment. It is freedom from attainment, freedom from the condition of one who attains, freedom from that whole process. So it is not by any of those outward signs that the Community is to be measured. It is by its adherence to its fundamental principle that the Community is recognized. As a practical matter, the Community consists of human beings in limitation by tendency. But it is continually fitted to the real principle of sadhana in which all of this is being undone. Outwardly, this Community appears like any other. There is no reason why you should think it has to look extraordinary. Be free of all of that. There is no reason you have to be extraordinary. Be ordinary, be happy.[3]

All this is not to say that the community is beyond criticism. There has been no more severe critic of the community than Da Love-Ananda himself. The Heart-Master's criticism, always tempered by love, is a form of benign purification. In fact, Da Love-Ananda has also been the community's greatest champion. Even his criticism only emphasizes the value that community life serves for spiritual practice:

DA LOVE-ANANDA: I urge you all to create community, to live cooperatively, and to make a culture out of

your association with one another, rather than merely
being a bunch of people who are individually studying the Teaching, perhaps practicing it in some way,
and who happen to associate with one another randomly and occasionally. A cooperative structure of
life is a profound aspect of spiritual practice. If this
practice does not achieve a cultural form in which
you all can live, the Way tends to get reduced to talk.

People relate to cooperative community as if it
were an unnecessary aspect of the practice, whereas
it is one of the most fundamental aspects of the
practice. If you understand this Teaching, you understand that the ego that is to be transcended exists
only in the context of relations. The ego is the body-
mind in the state of contraction. Therefore, it is
effective as contraction in the field of relations. And
therefore, the primary disciplines, the most fundamental disciplines, are in the domain of relations.

How, then, can you avoid the discipline of
community and imagine that you are practicing the
Way? How can you be reluctant merely because you
have difficulties with people? How can you be reluctant to enter into this discipline? Of course you have
difficulties with it! Difficulties are what you are all
about. [4]

One devotee tells the story of an event that included
some devotional singing. To his initial regret, he found himself beside a man with an extremely poor singing voice, who,
free of self-consciousness, belted out every song with great
enthusiasm at the top of his lungs. "In some ways," the
devotee relates, "it was awful. But his singing had so much
heart that he won me over. I would gladly have sung beside
him all night long!"

Even for mature practitioners life in spiritual community
is a challenging practice, accompanied by frustrations at times.
But those who are prepared for this mature practice discover
that, even in the midst of the difficulties that inevitably
confront anyone who enters into the discipline of community,

their appreciation of community life only grows stronger. The community has "so much heart" that its mutual love relationship with the Adept overshadows its obvious flaws. Before long, one becomes glad to add one's own unique voice to the song, even though at any given moment some of the singers, including oneself, may be off key.

CHAPTER FOURTEEN

The Vision of Mulund

In his first book, *The Knee of Listening,* Da Love-Ananda wrote: "I would find a new order of men who will create a new age of sanity and joy." [1] The organization that serves that new order, "The Vision of Mulund Association", takes its name from his experience at the end of his first trip to India in 1968.

On his way from Swami Muktananda's Ashram in Ganeshpuri to the airport in Bombay, Da Love-Ananda stayed overnight in the small town of Mulund, just outside Bombay. While still at the Ashram that morning, he had experienced his first occurrence of Conditional Nirvikalpa Samadhi, or the state in which body and mind and all objects of attention are utterly, though temporarily, transcended in the Divine Radiance perceived to be infinitely above the crown of the head. And in Mulund that night, he again entered into Nirvikalpa Samadhi.

The following morning, when Da Love-Ananda looked out from the roof of the house where he was staying, he saw Mulund transformed by his heightened, visionary state. The town itself was lovely and serene, and in the park below he saw men and women clothed with becoming simplicity walking at ease and enjoying leisure time with friends and family. His vision of this town captured the mood of relational Happiness that is his image of community life.

The Vision of Mulund Association, which serves the organization and management of the community of devotees, has now grown into a worldwide undertaking with local organizations in every region where devotees have gathered in significant numbers. Neither The Free Daist Communion nor The Vision of Mulund Association are identical to the sacred community itself, but both provide services to the body of practitioners. The Free Daist Communion, through its educational, cultural, and priestly services, provides the formal structure for the devotional life of the Communion, while The Vision of Mulund Association provides services in the areas of housing, businesses, schooling, health, and so on. The Association is made up of both individual practitioners and institutional organizations, such as The Vision of Mulund Institute and the Radiant Life Clinic.

The Vision of Mulund Institute was formed to create a school system and culture of learning for children. At present the Institute operates a pilot school system consisting of Big Wisdom Free School in northern California and The Garden of Lions, a boarding school in upstate New York. Other regional schools throughout the world also draw upon the Institute's resources and guidance.

The Radiant Life Clinic was founded in 1978 to develop the practice of Da Love-Ananda's Wisdom-Teaching as it applies to health and healing. Representatives of the Clinic serve each of the community's centers throughout the world. Although the Clinic provides some medical services, its primary focus is on education and research. Clinic staff present public seminars and lectures under the auspices of The Laughing Man Institute, which provides public education programs and educational and cultural services for beginning practitioners.

The community is comprised of people from all walks of life, including professionals, businessmen, and tradespeople. The community Businessmen's Association encourages students and practitioners to work together to develop an appropriate and right practice of business, harmonizing sound business principles with a spiritual Way of life. Additionally, the community includes several guilds of artisans, or groups of students and practitioners who work cooperatively to provide the sacred objects and traditional skills and services that enhance our sacred life together: Sacred Fires (those who

make sacred objects and articles of adornment), Seamless
Garment (the cooperative gathering of seamstresses), and
Inconceivable Mansions (the group of fine woodworkers).

In order for the community to fully manifest a complete
culture, all areas of life must be taken into account and
aligned to Da Love-Ananda's Wisdom. The community continues to develop responsibility for cooperative housing, cooperative businesses, childrearing, education, the arts, health,
sexuality and marriage, and so on. But more importantly, it
must come to encompass significant numbers of individuals in
the most advanced stages of practice, including the ultimate or
Enlightened stage. As this occurs, the complexion of the
community will change in ways that can hardly be predicted.

> DA LOVE-ANANDA: Such a Community has never existed.
> There have been groups that have gotten together for
> the sake of spiritual things, but they have not been
> Communities of Devotees in the perfect sense. Such
> a thing has never existed, never survived. The in-
> klings of it have developed in a few cases, around
> certain of the Siddhas [Adepts], but it has never
> become a living actuality. The Teaching was not full
> enough, the time was not right. So none of these
> communities ever truly became the Community of
> Devotees in the perfect sense. In this case the time is
> right, and the Teaching has been communicated in
> its fullness. There is no limitation on the Siddhi of
> God in this time, so the realization of this event
> depends entirely on your response.[2]

To respond to Da Love-Ananda's offering is the essential
purpose of the community of devotees. All other aspects of its
developing culture, although necessary in themselves, are
secondary to its fundamental principle: spiritual Communion
with the Transcendental Divine Being and Reality in the
spiritual Company of the God-Realized Heart-Master Da Love-
Ananda. Only through that practice does the community transcend the limits of the human condition, becoming an Agency
of the Divine. And only through the development of com-

munity can that Agency truly enter into the stream of human culture. In *The Dawn Horse Testament* Da Love-Ananda describes the vision of a true sacred community:

> Let Your Own body-mind and the body-minds Of My Other Devotees Serve As The psycho-physical Agents For My Blessing Work. Gather Together daily and Hear and See The Divine Person Together. Let each Be The Agent Of Reception For all others. [3]

SECTION FIVE

THE HOLY JUMPING-OFF PLACE:

*An Invitation to
the Way of the Heart*

*This is the secret of spiritual life: Love is God-
Communion, or freedom from fear. No
objective experience, no vision, no esoteric
structure or condition of any kind is God-
Realization, nor does any experience or condition
add to this Communion. The path itself is to be
love, to be unobstructed feeling-attention, to
persist in love under all conditions, and thereby to
transform the conditions of existence from that
point of view. If we abide in that Communion,
then all the conditions and possibilities of
existence are a great display of God that will
always be benign.*

Da Love-Ananda
The Way That I Teach, *pp. 63–64*

1986

CHAPTER FIFTEEN

You Must Wake Up!

a talk by Heart-Master Da Love-Ananda
May 11, 1977

D A LOVE-ANANDA: In fact and in Truth this manifest appearance in which we are animated to one another in the waking state is a hallucination that occurs in consciousness. All these trees, buildings, bodies, hairs, thoughts arise as modification of a single and absolute field that is Perfect Radiance. The world is a conception, as completely unnecessary as a thought or a dream. And it is just as silly, just as humorous, just as arbitrary and unserious, as any dream.

There is no need for this present configuration to appear. There is no reason for it to persist. There is no need to overcome it or to enjoy a victory as it. It is just as arbitrary as any dream you might have had recently. The dream came to an end—it became obsolete because you realized it was not necessary. You woke up.

You must be awake. Your awakening is what the communication of this Teaching is all about. The Teaching is a penetrating criticism, a goad to awakening to the non-necessity of things. The communication of Truth, the argument and Influence of the Spiritual Master, works to undermine the droning trance in which you exist in the waking state and in all other states of experience.

You ordinarily maintain the presumption of being this fleshy entity without the slightest ambiguity. That presumption just seems necessary. You do not feel that there is any way around it. You do not even regard the body to be something arising in consciousness. You consider consciousness to be somehow inside the body, in the brain, or in some condition less than the flesh itself, somehow created by senior unconscious atoms, its destiny determined by the fleshy thing that you know well. Thus, you presume that when you are dead, you are dead. But the necessity of the body is not true. This body is, presently, a hallucination in the field of brightness. When you can "see" that the body and the mind and the sense of separate identity itself all arise in the field of brightness as a mere modification, then you will have a great deal of humor relative to this affair of waking life. Then the great adventure of trying to attain a victory or to find the great goal for which all beings are born will come to an end. You will be free, but not until then. Until then, you are bound to discover, through all the means of release, some sort of extraordinary occasion that will console you as an entity.

The conventional spiritual teachings serve your search for consolation and reinforce the dilemma of existence. "Oh, Master, I'm suffering. What do I have to do to be saved? How do I get to heaven? How do I see God? How do I get to feel better?" And the master says, "Do this, do that, it is up here, it is in here, it is over there, it is to come, it is never realized." And so, on the the basis of your trouble, you are further motivated to feel good. Whereas the entire search, the entire drama of getting to Truth, is a lie. It is not true in this very moment that you are an entity. Your Condition is not that of an entity. The entity is only a convention of appearance. It is not Truth. That configuration is what is appearing, it is what is arising, but it is not the Truth in the moment.

In the present, and always in the past, and always in the future, the Condition of existence that is true and Truth is not defined and separate, but diffuse, without center or bounds. That is the Condition in this very moment. In that Condition, paradoxically, there arise all the conventions of limitation, out of which, in your ordinary impulse, you try to make your philosophy. You presume, on the basis of conventions of experiencing, what the universe must be like, what you are like, what your true Condition must be. But your Condition precedes all of experience. Your Condition is Wisdom, the force of Existence, which eternally precedes all this arising, and within which or as a modification of which this arising occurs. Only by realizing that Condition are you properly related to all these limitations that rise and fall, waking, dreaming, and sleeping, gross or subtle, in this world or any other world.

True awakening is penetration, in the present moment, of the presumption of the necessity and independence of your apparent or experienced condition. This penetration is not the same as the glamourous path of going within, of achieving a victorious subjectivity. That is the solution founded in the presumption of independence, of necessarily separate existence. Such a solution is a serious matter then. If you are separate, you must find some way to feel better while separate—to feel holy, to see lights, to feel blissful in some part—because life appears to be necessary and humorless, a dilemma to be undone. The whole universe, then, becomes a problem and an always contradicted adventure, a game that you can win or lose, a very treacherous and fundamentally unhappy affair.

If you will observe all the human beings you casually meet, you will see that basically they are tormented by their existence. They are presuming their independence presently, and, therefore, they suffer all the effects of the drama, the play, the conjunction of apparent entities and processes. This life is treacherous, humorless, bearing down on them, drawing them into a destiny upon which they can have no ultimate effect. They can perhaps produce modest little effects, but they cannot ultimately be relieved of the dilemma that impinges on them.

This dilemma, however, is only their presumption and it is false. The force of their birth implies their independence, and they meditate on that separation constantly. Thus, they look for their release in the context of presumed separation. Instead of being released, however, they are burdened, impinged upon by endless effects. Furthermore, the thing they most identify with, that born, vital body-being, is disintegrating over time, getting worse and worse, and eventually dying.

No wonder people get more and more solemn as the years go on.

What you know of dreams should illumine your position in the waking state. You are in exactly the same position in the waking state as in the dream state. You know very well, from the point of view of the waking state, that in dreaming you create the environment as well as the sense of being an independent entity. Clearly the dream is your own consciousness. It is your dream. Who else made the dream but you? It arises in your own consciousness. If, in the dream, you are running to leap into the water and suddenly it turns into a pit of fire, you created it. Your own psychic nature made the fire, so that you fell into fire instead of swimming over the lake. This is clear when you wake up, though it is not clear in the dream itself, because in the dream you identify exclusively with the knowing entity, the ego presumption, the separate one in the adventure. When you wake, you realize that you created all of it, that it was your own consciousness, and that now, in the waking state, it has no necessity. Now it is completely arbitrary, a hallucination. You must wake up! Not a single thought, conception, or experience, high or low, is anything but a permutation of the dream. Only the awakening itself, in which there is nothing happening, is liberation from the motivated distress of all things happening.

In that awakening, no matter what arises, in any moment, you do not suffer the apparent logic or implications of appearances, but remain established in your real Condition, which is the unqualified field of Radiant Consciousness, without center and without bounds. From the Radiance of that Consciousness all things arise as vibratory modifications, including the most solid things that you consider to be objective to you as the knower-I. If you realize the true Condition of the knower-I, you also realize the true Condition of all manifestation. It is hallucination, the conjunction of wave patterns, appearing very elusive to vision at times, and then at another moment defining their lines into rigid object.

Yet there are no independent objects. There are no truly solid things. This world is a phenomenon of light. If you have studied contemporary physics, you have at least heard and thought this, but you have not yet realized its full implications. This world, and every sense of subjective or objective independence, is a phenomenon of light, a hallucination. It is always an event in the very Condition that is consciousness, the unqualified field of which everything that arises is the present modification. If you presume the condition or effect of any modification, rather than That in which the modification arises, then that effect becomes necessary, and the presumption that it is your Condition reinforces a complex adventure in which you are this implied knower-I, separate from events. But if you break through that presumption and if you are presently existing as the prior, diffuse, or absolute Condition, then the arising phenomena have a paradoxical significance. They are unnecessary, they are humorous, they are fluid, they are not binding. The whole adventure they imply, negative or positive, is unnecessary, untrue. Everything that arises, subjective or objective, is a portion of the dream. It has nothing in itself to do with God or Truth. Truth is realized only in the right presumption in the present, regardless of what arises. It is the tacit certainty that this is a completely unnecessary hallucination, a modification of light.

You must begin to stand in your real position, the true Condition in this moment, before all the belief systems, all the implications of the solid, present dream, enforce themselves as your presumption. You do not know what a single thing is. Not a single thing! Not even the subjective part that is saying to itself, "I do not know what the wall is, I do not know what a single thing is." You do not know what the thoughts are, you do not know what the feelings are, you do not know what this "I" is! "I" is the whole body in fact, but there is no knowledge of what the body is entirely and independently and absolutely. You do not know what anything is. Therefore, you do not know what all things are. The whole of manifestation altogether is not a something of which you are a knower. You are Ignorance. You are a most undefined or diffuse Condition, unable to radically differentiate yourself from a single thing, because as long as any single thing arises, you exist in the vulnerable position of having no knowledge of what it is.

You are already without form, without a foundation, without anything solid to rest on. You do not rest up against anything. You are not deeply behind or within anything. You are completely vulnerable and an absolute Mystery. You live in Mystery. When you have considered that fact to the point of hearing, to the point that this Mystery becomes tolerable and you are not grasping so mightily onto egoic consolations, but are able to move into relations with some ease—having heard me to that degree, then you can meet me in the spiritual sense. Then you begin to become sensitive to my Company, and then meeting me becomes a spiritual occasion that draws you more and more profoundly into this Realization of the present Condition.

That is what there is to realize in my Company. It is this profound initiation into our Condition in this moment. Until in your sympathy with me you begin to realize it most directly, all I can do is witness to you that I (and, therefore, you and all beings) am not identical to the condition of being a separate entity. I am not an entity: I am not inside a body. To call myself this body is just as arbitrary as to say I am the morning star or the vision within or a light you may see by turning upward. These are all arbitrary identifications, completely unnecessary, completely humorous, completely without the slightest bit of seriousness from my point of view.

Ultimately, it becomes clear that the tree in the yard is a hallucination, that it is a matter of mind, just as any thought that you project inwardly. It is exactly the same. You will not at last have to go through a mental process to believe this. It will just appear to be obviously that way. And when it is obvious, it is not disorienting. The presumption of our real Condition is neither a thought nor an act. It is not itself a state of experience, gross or subtle. It is a kind of transparency. The present appearance is simply a process arising in a Condition that is without center, form, relations, or bounds. That Condition is transparent, obvious, and the only presumption that is Truth or Happiness. Until it is obvious, you must listen, you must hear, you must engage the argument, you must presume the disciplines. The practice of the Way is leading toward this Realization absolutely.

Consider the argument and live the discipline. There will be a fire in that discipline equal to the degree of frustration of your habitual presumptions and distractions. Allow that fire to enter into this consideration, and it will be the undoing of this ordinary presumption of independence and necessity that seems so perfectly natural and logical to you in this hallucination, this dream, this birth. You will begin to penetrate that presumption, and its logic will no longer bind you.

You must take up this Way as a whole life. Just sitting here with whatever attention you have freely available at the moment is not sufficient to change your presumption in the future. It will simply establish you in the moment, more or less, in this consideration of Ignorance. But the discipline is obliged upon you in every moment. You must take it up as a way of life. You must be constantly available to the Spiritual Master, constantly available to his instruction, his argument, his disciplines, his Company. The life awakened in his Company serves the penetration of the dream. When that Realization becomes summary, most radical, in your case, then you are simply happy. Until then, you enjoy it more or less profoundly in some moments, and at other moments the usual life grinds in on you. But then you have the discipline to occupy you rather than the right you ordinarily assume to dramatize your self-possessed tendencies and illusions. The whole affair of this practice ultimately serves perfect transformation in Truth.

Difficulties persist because the ordinary life or dream persists. Things continue to arise. So there is heat in the process. But the heat is your advantage. The heat is not some negative side effect. The heat is free attention, available for this profundity. Secondarily, it is painful in a sense, but it is free. It is available force, attention. Free attention is not otherwise so available, because it is usually sunk into dramatizations and distractions. Now it is without an object. It cannot find a way to be relieved. It is hot. And so it can consider itself, the occasion itself.

If, through true hearing, you will be committed to such present consideration, and if you will persist in it and not restrain yourself from the whole discipline of my Company, that same Enlightenment that is now argued to your face will also be true of you.

CHAPTER SIXTEEN

Jumping Off

For Your Continued Practice of Listening

When Da Love-Ananda was a young boy, on outings when his father was driving the car, they would at times approach the top of a hill, beyond which they could see nothing but empty space. As they neared the apparent drop-off and the earth rushed away before them, at the most dramatic point, his father would gesture into the looming emptiness, saying "There it is—the holy jumping-off place!"

Ultimately, Enlightenment or God-Realization requires a great leap—the transcendence of everything, holding on to nothing. The practice of spiritual life before Enlightenment can be seen as preparation for that supreme moment of crisis at the holy jumping-off place. In truth, each moment of real spiritual practice involves the same leap of self-transcendence. To embrace a spiritual Way of life is to arrive at the holy jumping-off place over and over again.

This book serves as only the briefest introduction, a "jumping-off" place, to the Way of the Heart offered by Heart-Master Da Love-Ananda. In the course of his Teaching Work, Da Love-Ananda generated over thirty volumes of published literature. Of those many volumes, he singled out five as the major "source texts" of his Teaching Word: *The Dawn Horse Testament, The Knee of Listening, The Method of the Siddhas,*

Love-Ananda Gita, and *The Illusion Of Relatedness.*

The Dawn Horse Testament is the culminating volume of Da Love-Ananda's sixteen years of Teaching Work with students and practitioners. In it he sets forth in summary form and in practical detail all the essential 'aspects of the Way of the Heart. He covers every aspect of spiritual practice from its inception to ultimate Self-Realization, including the esoteric "secrets" of the advanced stages of practice and the higher physics of the process of Enlightenment.

The Dawn Horse Testament is Da Love-Ananda's "Eternal Conversation", his summary Teaching Word on the ancient Way of Communion with the Living Divine Reality. Da Love-Ananda said: "This Testament is my Intention to Awaken the Transcendental Self of every being to the Real Divine Condition."

The Knee of Listening: The Early Life and Radical Spiritual Teachings of Franklin Jones [Heart-Master Da Love-Ananda] (published in 1972) is Da Love-Ananda's first published book and an essential statement of his Wisdom-Teaching, containing an autobiographical account of his own Ordeal of Realization and essays on the practice and Realization of the Way of the Heart. Written immediately after the culminating events of his Re-Awakening to the Transcendental Self, Da Love-Ananda's life history serves as an example and lesson for all who take up the Way of the Heart. It is a remarkable account of the sudden transformative experiences he endured, his unusual relationship to his Teachers, and his discovery of the radical process of the transcendence of the ego or self-contraction.

The Method of the Siddhas: Talks with Franklin Jones [Heart-Master Da Love-Ananda] on the Spiritual Technique of the Saviors of Mankind is the second of Da Love-Ananda's published books. Published in 1973, it documents the first year of his Teaching Work through talks with devotees during 1972–73. Addressing the questions and problems of the ordinary people who first came to him, Da Love-Ananda speaks about the technical practices of the Way of the Heart as well as the practices of other traditions. But the essential communication of the book is the great process that unfolds in relationship to the Heart-Master, whose fundamental message then as today is the necessity of "Satsang", "the Company of Truth".

In the *Love-Ananda Gita: The Free-Song of Love-Bliss*, unique in the long history of religious and spiritual communication, Da Love-Ananda speaks only from the disposition of Enlightenment itself rather than addressing the earlier stages of spiritual practice. Its radical message, embodying the pure Wisdom of the Awakened Heart, stands as an inspiration and an example to all who would embrace a God-Realizing Way of life. This book was written in 1986.

The Illusion Of Relatedness, written in 1986 during Da Love-Ananda's "last Submission as Teacher", appeals to every reader to Realize God directly by "hearing" (or understanding) his Teaching Argument, by "seeing" the Image of Happiness hidden in every heart, and by "practicing" the Way that he has Revealed—the Way of self-transcending devotion to and Realization of the Divine Person, the Only One Who Is. Arising from Da Love-Ananda's compassionate struggle on behalf of all who suffer the chains of egoity, this book presents the Way of Freedom in the most clear and practical terms.

The Dawn Horse Testament, The Knee of Listening, and *The Method of the Siddhas* are all excellent next books for those interested in studying the Wisdom-Teaching of Da Love-Ananda in more detail. The books described in the "Listening" section of "The Written and Spoken Teaching Word of Heart-Master Da Love-Ananda" (see pp. 145–53 of this volume) are also very useful introductions to his Wisdom-Teaching.

Those who look forward to hearing Da Love-Ananda's voice in his recorded talks will enjoy the audiotapes "The Bodily Location of Happiness", "Feeling without Limitation", and "God Is Not in Charge".

In "The Bodily Location of Happiness", a talk given to some three hundred students and practitioners on November 28, 1981, Da Love-Ananda reveals the means by which Happiness may be located through self-understanding and surrender to the Divine. He makes clear the double bind we create for ourselves in our frenetic seeking for Happiness—for our seeking itself is actually a commitment to unhappiness. Instead of assuming our unhappiness, we should locate our present Happiness through the process of feeling-surrender that he describes. The location of Happiness, he says, should become a profound practice in daily life as well as in meditation.

In "Feeling without Limitation" Da Love-Ananda argues that we are always placing limits on feeling. Feeling, he says, is not just a matter of emotion—it is the Feeling of Being that encompasses the total body-mind. In this talk, given on May 24, 1983, Da Love-Ananda draws us into an understanding of our responsibility for our own suffering—our contraction from full Feeling. Only this self-understanding awakens the motive to self-transcendence, the impulse toward Feeling without limitation, or Love-Bliss.

"God Is Not in Charge" consists of two talks, given on September 2–3, 1982, and February 2, 1984. Da Love-Ananda brings great humor and insight to a discussion of popular religious misconceptions about the nature of the Divine. He clarifies the "problem" that the great unhappiness and suffering in the world present to the conventional religious mind. In a very lively and playful mood, he criticizes the presumption of a childish relationship to a Divine "father" who "takes care of you", and shows how this view of the Divine is in fact the root of religious cultism.

The talk "The Bodily Location of Happiness" is also available on videotape, which adds another dimension to Da Love-Ananda's recorded speech, for the bodily gestures and facial expressions of the Heart-Master communicate his Condition more powerfully than any words. Many people find these videotapes to be the most rewarding and enjoyable presentation of his Teaching Word.

In the video recording of "The Fire Must Have Its Way", given on July 17, 1978, Da Love-Ananda describes the often difficult and always intense practice of true spiritual life, which, like a fire, both purifies and Enlightens the devotee. In traditional spiritual symbolism, fire represents both the spiritual process and the feeling dimension of existence. This dual significance reflects the truth revealed by Heart-Master Da Love-Ananda that God is absolute or unqualified Feeling. And to practice the God-Realizing Way is to Awaken to the realization that you can feel absolutely, that you can be Ecstatic, Blissful, completely Happy, and Free.

For a complete listing of the books and tapes of Heart-Master Da Love-Ananda, please see "The Written and Spoken Teaching Word of Heart-Master Da Love-Ananda" on page 145 of this volume.

Events Sponsored by The Laughing Man Institute

If you would like to find out more about Da Love-Ananda's life and Work, The Laughing Man Institute offers introductory programs and courses at its public centers around the world as well as many services for people not living within easy access of a center. Introductory videotapes are shown frequently at every public center. Write or call the Regional Center nearest you to receive a printed bimonthly calendar of events in your area. (A list of the Regional Centers and their associated study groups appears on pp. 139–41.)

"The Glorious Option", a full-day introductory seminar of experiential exercises, illustrates key themes of the Way of the Heart. Participants in the seminar enjoy accounts of Da Love-Ananda's transformative Work with students and practitioners as well as videotapes of talks given by Da Love-Ananda. Additionally, participants will have the opportunity to ask questions about the Way of the Heart in a small group setting. (This seminar is a prerequisite for becoming a student of The Laughing Man Institute.)

The Area Study-Group Program

If you live at a distance from our Regional Centers, nearly sixty Area Study Groups are now meeting formally to enjoy videotapes and recorded talks by Heart-Master Da Love-Ananda and mature practitioners, and to participate in guided study of the Way. To locate the study group near you, contact your Regional Center for more information.

The Home-Study Course

For newcomers and longtime readers of the Wisdom-Teaching of Da Love-Ananda, the home-study course entitled "Listen To Me and Hear Me" systematically introduces in a lively and concentrated form Da Love-Ananda's Wisdom-Teaching on Satsang (or the Company of Truth), Narcissus (or the activity of self-contraction), Understanding, Happiness, and Divine Ignorance. The course is also designed to accompany study of *The Dawn Horse Testament* and other primary texts. Monthly lessons feature excerpts from talks and essays by Da Love-Ananda, carefully selected to address the initial questions and concerns of those studying the Way. Subscribers also have the opportunity to correspond with practitioners in The Free Daist Communion. And included with every other monthly lesson is an audiotape that guides the listener through the meditative contemplation of an essential aspect of Da Love-Ananda's Teaching Argument.

The Friends Program

Those who are already appreciative of Da Love-Ananda's Work and who wish to acknowledge their support of the Way of the Heart are invited to join the growing circle of Friends of The Laughing Man Institute.

Formal Friends enjoy access to a broad range of special educational and cultural programs. Longtime practitioners of the Way of the Heart offer weekly courses of intensive, guided study of such key texts as *The Knee of Listening, The Method of the Siddhas,* and *The Dawn Horse Testament.* Friends and invited guests also gather as often as every two months for "Celebrations of Good Company". Celebrations generally include recent communications of the Blessing Work of Da Love-Ananda, audio-video recordings, guided pondering of the Wisdom-Teaching, and opportunities to meet and talk with students of the Way.

Periodic weekend retreats for Friends and beginning students are also offered in many Regions, featuring instruction in conscious exercise, guided meditation, and in-depth considerations of questions about the Way of the Heart.

Friends simply contribute $100 annually in support of the public work of the Institute, and they are welcome to engage and receive instruction in the practice of "pondering" the Teaching Word of Heart-Master Da Love-Ananda. Every Friend receives a complimentary one-year subscription to *The Laughing Man* magazine, which communicates the Wisdom-Teaching of Heart-Master Da Love-Ananda and critically introduces what Da Love-Ananda terms the "Great Tradition" of philosophy, religion, and spirituality. Friends also enjoy discounts on most seminars, retreats, and topical lectures offered by The Laughing Man Institute. Finally, Friends are invited to subscribe to *Crazy Wisdom,* the journal available exclusively to Friends, students, and practitioners. *Crazy Wisdom* chronicles Da Love-Ananda's Blessing Work, and features talks and essays by Heart-Master Da Love-Ananda, interviews and articles by devotees, and cultural news from the worldwide fellowship of practitioners.

Becoming a Student in The Laughing Man Institute

If you wish to consider actual practice of the Way of the Heart (and you have already attended the "Glorious Option" seminar), we offer a pre-student course entitled "The Way of Divine Grace", an eight-week course on the formal practices and obligations of a student in The Laughing Man Institute. Pre-students consider their motivation to undertake spiritual life and apply themselves to the Teaching-Argument. Each participant has the opportunity to consider the futility of the ego's search for consolation, and to magnify his or her own intuition of the Divine Happiness that is already the "prior Condition" of everyone.

Because the Wisdom-Teaching of Heart-Master Da Love-Ananda can be validated only in each person's own experience, we invite all to approach the Way of the Heart first through his Teaching-Argument. The Wisdom-Teaching turns the heart of the listener to self-understanding, so that he or she may transcend all commitments to the unhappy ordeal of seeking and ultimately receive the Spirit-Blessing of God, the Divine Person or Reality.

For More Information about
The Laughing Man Institute

The Laughing Man Institute cordially invites you to choose the form of involvement most appropriate to your present level of response. For more information about public seminars, retreats, and courses, the Friends program, or the area study groups, please call or write the Regional Center nearest you, or write:

The Laughing Man Institute
P.O. Box 12775
San Rafael, CA 94913-2775 U.S.A.

The Regional Centers of
The Laughing Man Institute

If you wish to participate in the Laughing Man Institute programs in your area, please contact the Regional Center nearest you (listed below*), or contact:

The Laughing Man Institute
750 Adrian Way, Suite 111
San Rafael, CA 94903, U.S.A.
(415) 492-9382

NORTHERN CALIFORNIA
740 Adrian Way
San Rafael, CA 94903
(415) 492-0930

Northern California Area Groups
Berkeley, California
Nevada City, California
Sacramento, California
San Francisco, California
Santa Cruz, California
Santa Rosa, California
Sunnyvale, California

SOUTHERN CALIFORNIA
616 Santa Monica Blvd., Suite 218
Santa Monica, CA 90401
(213) 393-1953

Southern California/Southwest U.S.A. Area Groups
Phoenix, Arizona
Tucson, Arizona
Denver, Colorado
Longmont, Colorado
Albuquerque, New Mexico

* This list is current as of fall 1986.

SOUTH CENTRAL U.S.A.
12501 Esplanade (P.O. Box 202438)
Austin, Texas 78720-2430
(512) 835-5167

South Central U.S.A. Area Groups
Houston, Texas
Leander, Texas
New Orleans, Louisiana

NORTHWEST U.S.A.
918 N.E. 64th St.
Seattle, WA 98115
(206) 527-0260

Northwestern U.S.A./Western Canada Area Groups
Calgary (Alberta), Canada
Vancouver (B.C.), Canada
Winnipeg (Manitoba), Canada
Ketchum, Idaho
Eugene, Oregon
Portland, Oregon
Ogden, Utah

NORTHEAST U.S.A.
P.O. Box 6
Auburndale, MA 02166
(617) 965-9711

Northeastern U.S.A. Area Groups
Amherst, Massachusetts
Brighton, Massachusetts
Cape Cod, Massachusetts
Dalton, Massachusetts
Springfield, Massachusetts
West Orange, New Jersey
Hudson Falls, New York

Islip, New York
Kew Gardens, New York
Mt. Kisco, New York
Bethlehem, Pennsylvania
Philadelphia, Pennsylvania
Richmond, Vermont

MIDWEST U.S.A.
59 Country Club Ct.
Palatine, Illinois 60067
(312) 934-3089
(312) 934-5609

Midwestern U.S.A. Area Groups
St. Louis, Illinois
Western Springs, Illinois
New Albany, Indiana
Ann Arbor, Michigan
Charlevoix, Michigan
Grove City, Ohio

SOUTHEAST U.S.A.
6516 Western Ave.
Chevy Chase, Maryland 20815
(301) 656-6867

Southeastern U.S.A. Area Groups
Jacksonville, Florida
St. Petersburg, Florida
Atlanta, Georgia
Lexington, Kentucky
Raleigh, North Carolina

EASTERN CANADA
88 Owen Blvd.
Willowdale, Ontario M2P 1G3
Canada
(416) 733-1822

Eastern Canada Area Groups
Montreal (Quebec), Canada
Ottawa (Ontario), Canada

THE UNITED KINGDOM AND IRELAND
28-A Poland Street
London W1V 3DB
England
01-734-4217

The United Kingdom and Ireland Area Groups
Manchester, England
Dublin, Ireland

THE NETHERLANDS
Prinsengracht 719
1017JW Amsterdam
The Netherlands
20-277600

NEW ZEALAND
21 High Street
CPO Box 3185
Auckland 1
New Zealand
09-390032

New Zealand Area Groups
Christchurch, New Zealand
Wellington, New Zealand

AUSTRALIA-MELBOURNE
163 Russell St., 1st floor
Melbourne, Victoria 3001
Australia
03-663-5305

Australia-Melbourne Area Groups
Perth, Australia
Adelaide, Australia

AUSTRALIA-SYDNEY
21 Coolaroo Road
Lane Cove, New South Wales
Australia 20066
613-384-949

Australia-Sydney Area Groups
Byron, Australia

HAWAII, MEXICO, and HONG KONG Area Groups
For information on these groups, contact The Laughing Man Institute, 750 Adrian Way, San Rafael, CA 94903 U.S.A., or phone (415) 492-9382.
Honolulu, Hawaii
Lihue, Hawaii
Chiapas, Mexico

NOTES

All the references below are from the works of Heart-Master Da Love-Ananda, published by The Dawn Horse Press, San Rafael, California. For a complete listing of Da Love-Ananda's recorded Teaching, please see "The Written and Spoken Teaching Word of Heart-Master Da Love-Ananda" on p. 145 of this volume.

CHAPTER ONE

1. *The Knee of Listening,* pp. 9–10.

2. *Vision Mound,* vol. 2, no. 5, p. 7.

3. *The Knee of Listening,* pp. 134–35.

4. *The Enlightenment of the Whole Body,* p. 38.

CHAPTER THREE

1. *The Dawn Horse Testament Of Heart-Master Da Free John [Heart-Master Da Love-Ananda],* p. 74.

2. *Easy Death,* pp. 379–80.

3. *The Paradox of Instruction,* p. 29.

4. *The Dreaded Gom-Boo, or the Imaginary Disease That Religion Seeks to Cure,* pp. 116–17.

5. *The Dawn Horse Testament,* pp. 126–27.

6. *The Paradox of Instruction,* p. 95.

CHAPTER FOUR

1. *The Knee of Listening,* p. 26.

2. *The Method of the Siddhas,* pp. 217–18, 220, 221.

3. From an unpublished talk by Heart-Master Da Love-Ananda, December 17, 1982.

4. *The Dawn Horse Testament,* p. 113.

5. *The Fire Gospel,* pp. 107–108.

6. *The Dawn Horse Testament,* p. 129.

CHAPTER FIVE

1. *The Dawn Horse Testament,* pp. 269–70.

2. *Do You Know What Anything Is?* pp. 124–32.

CHAPTER EIGHT

1. *Garbage and the Goddess,* pp. xvii–xviii.

2. *Crazy Wisdom,* vol. 2, no. 4 (July 1983), pp. 3–4.

3. *The Bodily Location of Happiness,* pp. 84–85.

4. From an unpublished talk by Heart-Master Da Love-Ananda, October 27, 1984.

5. *Bodily Worship of the Living God,* p. 159.

CHAPTER TEN

1. *Scientific Proof of the Existence of God Will Soon Be Announced by the White House!* pp. 365–66.

2. *The Transmission of Doubt*, pp. 413–15.

3. *The Dreaded Gom-Boo, or the Imaginary Disease That Religion Seeks to Cure*, pp. 116–17.

4. *The Bodily Location of Happiness*, p. 193.

5. *The Transmission of Doubt*, pp. 298–99.

6. *The Bodily Sacrifice of Attention*, pp. 17–18.

7. *What Is the Conscious Process?* p. 28.

CHAPTER ELEVEN

1. From an unpublished talk by Heart-Master Da Love-Ananda, July 17, 1978.

CHAPTER TWELVE

1. From an unpublished talk by Heart-Master Da Love-Ananda, March 16, 1986.

CHAPTER THIRTEEN

1. *No Remedy*, p. 55.

2. *Garbage and the Goddess*, p. 332.

3. Ibid., p. 336.

4. *Crazy Wisdom*, vol. 1, no. 12 (March 1983), pp. 6, 9.

CHAPTER FOURTEEN

1. *The Knee of Listening*, p. 242.

2. *Garbage and the Goddess*, p. 228.

3. *The Dawn Horse Testament,*, p. 336

The Written and Spoken Teaching Word of Heart-Master Da Love-Ananda

THE SOURCE LITERATURE

These source books are the epitome of Heart-Master Da Love-Ananda's Wisdom-Teaching on the attributes, secrets, and Realization of the Heart, or Radiant Transcendental Consciousness.

THE DAWN HORSE TESTAMENT
Of Heart-Master Da Free John [Heart-Master Da Love-Ananda]
$45.00 cloth, $12.95 paper

THE KNEE OF LISTENING
The Early Life and Radical Spiritual Teaching of Franklin Jones [Heart-Master Da Love-Ananda]
$10.95 paper

THE METHOD OF THE SIDDHAS
Talks with Franklin Jones [Heart-Master Da Love-Ananda] on the Spiritual Technique of the Saviors of Mankind
$11.95 paper

LOVE-ANANDA GITA
The Free-Song of Love-Bliss
$10.95 cloth

THE ILLUSION OF RELATEDNESS
Essays on True and Free Renunciation and the Radical Transcendence of Conditional Existence
$8.95 paper

THE PRACTICAL TEXTS

The following practical texts elaborate the basic life-disciplines practiced in the Way of the Heart.

THE EATING GORILLA COMES IN PEACE
The Transcendental Principle of Life Applied to Diet and the
Regenerative Discipline of True Health
$12.95 paper

RAW GORILLA
The Principles of Regenerative Raw Diet Applied in True
Spiritual Practice
$3.95 paper

CONSCIOUS EXERCISE AND THE TRANSCENDENTAL SUN
The principle of love applied to exercise and the method of
common physical action. A science of whole body wisdom, or
true emotion, intended most especially for those engaged in
religious or spiritual life.
$8.95 paper

LOVE OF THE TWO-ARMED FORM
The Free and Regenerative Function of Sexuality in Ordinary
Life, and the Transcendence of Sexuality in True Religious or
Spiritual Practice
$12.95 paper

MANUALS OF PRACTICE

The manuals of practice are listed below according to the stages of the development of the Way of the Heart Revealed by Heart-Master Da Love-Ananda. The Way begins with "listening" to the message of the Teaching Word until true "hearing" or understanding of his Argument awakens. Then "seeing", emotional conversion, or love of the Divine Person and Presence, follows. On the basis of "hearing" and "seeing", true "practice" of the Way begins. The manuals of practice can usefully be studied not only by practitioners but by anyone interested in the Way of the Heart.

LISTENING to the Argument of Truth

These books serve the concentrated study and pondering of Da Love-Ananda's Fundamental Questions and Teaching Arguments relative to "Narcissus" (or the self-contraction), "Radical Understanding" (or direct feeling-transcendence of the self-contraction), and "Divine Ignorance" (or intuition of Radiant Transcendental Consciousness).

THE HOLY JUMPING-OFF PLACE
An Introduction to the Way of the Heart Revealed by Heart-Master Da Love-Ananda
$5.95 paper

THE FOUR FUNDAMENTAL QUESTIONS
Talks and essays about human experience and the actual practice of an Enlightened Way of Life
$2.95 paper

SCIENTIFIC PROOF OF THE EXISTENCE OF GOD WILL SOON BE ANNOUNCED BY THE WHITE HOUSE!
Prophetic Wisdom about the Myths and Idols of mass culture and popular religious cultism, the new priesthood of scientific and political materialism, and the secrets of Enlightenment hidden in the body of Man
$12.95 paper

DO YOU KNOW WHAT ANYTHING IS?
Talks and Essays on Divine Ignorance
$6.95 paper

THE ADEPT
Selections from Talks and Essays by Da Free John [Heart-Master Da Love-Ananda] on the Nature and Function of the Enlightened Teacher
$4.95 paper

THE GOD IN EVERY BODY BOOK
Talks and Essays on God-Realization
$3.95 paper

THE TRANSMISSION OF DOUBT
Talks and Essays on the Transcendence of Scientific Materialism through Radical Understanding
$10.95

ENLIGHTENMENT AND THE TRANSFORMATION OF MAN
Selections from Talks and Essays on the Spiritual Process and God-Realization
$7.95

THE YOGA OF CONSIDERATION AND THE WAY
THAT I TEACH
*Talks and Essays on the distinction between preliminary
practices and the radical Way of prior Enlightenment*
$7.95 paper

THE TRANSCENDENCE OF EGO AND EGOIC SOCIETY
(booklet)
$2.00

A CALL FOR THE RADICAL REFORMATION OF CHRISTIANITY
(booklet)
$2.00

SCIENCE, SACRED CULTURE, AND REALITY (booklet)
$2.50

HEARING and Understanding the Truth

Da Love-Ananda makes clear that before true practice of
the Way can begin, "hearing" must unlock the heart and
awaken the motive toward self-transcending God-Realization
and the Recognition of the Divine Person and Presence.

THE DREADED GOM-BOO, OR THE IMAGINARY DISEASE
THAT RELIGION SEEKS TO CURE
*A Collection of Essays and Talks on the "Direct" Process of
Enlightenment*
$9.95 paper

THE WAY THAT I TEACH
Talks on the Intuition of Eternal Life
$14.95 cloth

THE BODILY SACRIFICE OF ATTENTION
*Introductory Talks on Radical Understanding and the Life of
Divine Ignorance*
$10.95 paper

WHAT IS THE CONSCIOUS PROCESS?
*Talks and essays on the tacit intuition of Transcendental
Consciousness, being a summary consideration of the Way of
Radical Understanding or Divine Ignorance*
$8.95 paper

SEEING and the Process of Spiritual Baptism

Real practice of the Way is founded on "seeing", or Spirit-Baptism, which is the process of emotional conversion to and Communion with the Spiritual Presence of the Divine. Seeing is principally initiated and developed through the esoteric process of reception of the Transmission of Happiness that is always available in the Spiritual Company of the Heart-Master.

BODILY WORSHIP OF THE LIVING GOD
The Esoteric Practice of Prayer Taught by Da Free John [Heart-Master Da Love-Ananda]
$10.95 paper

COMPULSORY DANCING
Talks and Essays on the spiritual and evolutionary necessity of emotional surrender to the Life-Principle
$3.95 paper

THE FIRE GOSPEL
Essays and Talks on Spiritual Baptism
$8.95 paper

"I" IS THE BODY OF LIFE
Talks and Essays on the Art and Science of Equanimity and the Self-Transcending Process of Radical Understanding
$10.95 paper

SPIRITUAL TRANSMISSION AND SELF-SURRENDER (booklet)
$3.00

PRACTICE and Realization of the Way

The manuals listed below describe the mature practice of the Way that begins once the foundations of "hearing" and "seeing" are stable. With the source texts, these books comprise Heart-Master Da Love-Ananda's published instructions on the practice and fulfillment of the Way of the Heart.

THE HYMN OF THE MASTER
A Confessional Recitation on the Mystery of the Spiritual Master based on the principal verses of the Guru Gita *(freely selected, rendered, and adapted by Da Free John [Heart-Master Da Love-Ananda])*
$9.95 paper

THE BODILY LOCATION OF HAPPINESS
On the Incarnation of the Divine Person and the Transmission of Love-Bliss
$8.95 paper

THE ENLIGHTENMENT OF THE WHOLE BODY
A Rational and New Prophetic Revelation of the Truth of Religion, Esoteric Spirituality, and the Divine Destiny of Man
$14.95 paper

THE PARADOX OF INSTRUCTION
An Introduction to the Esoteric Spiritual Teaching of Bubba Free John [Heart-Master Da Love-Ananda]
$14.95 cloth

NIRVANASARA
Radical Transcendentalism and the Introduction of Advaitayana Buddhism
$9.95 paper

THE LIBERATOR (ELEUTHERIOS)
$12.95 cloth, $6.95 paper
The summary of Da Love-Ananda's instructions on "the Perfect Practice", or the Ultimate Practice of the Way.

EASY DEATH
Talks and Essays on the Inherent and Ultimate Transcendence of Death and Everything Else
$10.95 paper

FOR AND ABOUT CHILDREN

WHAT TO REMEMBER TO BE HAPPY
A Spiritual Way of Life for Your First Fourteen Years or So
$4.95 paper

I AM HAPPINESS
A Rendering for Children of the Spiritual Adventure of Master Da Free John [Heart-Master Da Love-Ananda]
Adapted by Daji Bodha and Lynne Closser from The Knee of Listening *by Master Da Free John [Heart-Master Da Love-Ananda]*
$8.95 paper

LOOK AT THE SUNLIGHT ON THE WATER
Educating Children for a Life of Self-Transcending Love and Happiness
$7.95 paper

INSPIRATIONAL AND DEVOTIONAL TEXTS

CRAZY DA MUST SING, INCLINED TO HIS WEAKER SIDE
Confessional Poems of Liberation and Love by the "Western" Adept, Da Free John [Heart-Master Da Love-Ananda]
$6.95 paper

FOREHEAD, BREATH, AND SMILE
An Anthology of Devotional Readings from the Spiritual Teaching of Master Da Free John [Heart-Master Da Love-Ananda]
$20.95 cloth

GOD IS NOT A GENTLEMAN AND I AM THAT ONE
Ecstatic Talks on Conventional Foolishness versus the Crazy Wisdom of God-Realization
$6.95 paper

PERIODICALS

THE LAUGHING MAN magazine
The Alternative to Scientific Materialism and Religious Provincialism
2 issues, $12.95

CRAZY WISDOM magazine
The Journal of The Free Daist Communion
(Available only to formal Friends, students, and practitioners of the Way of the Heart) 6 issues, $36.00

CASSETTE TAPES:

The recorded ecstatic speech of Da Love-Ananda ($9.95 each):

THE BODILY LOCATION OF HAPPINESS

FEELING WITHOUT LIMITATION

OF THIS I AM PERFECTLY CERTAIN
Ecstatic Readings by Da Free John

I AM THE HEART OF MAN
*A Recitation by Heart-Master Da Free John [Heart-Master Da
Love-Ananda]*

VIDEOTAPES OF HEART-MASTER
DA LOVE-ANANDA'S TALKS

THE BODILY LOCATION OF HAPPINESS
$59.95, 56 minutes, VHS format

THE FIRE MUST HAVE ITS WAY
$59.95, 57 minutes, VHS format

Available at local bookstores and by mail from

THE DAWN HORSE BOOK DEPOT
P. O. Box 15260
Seattle, WA 98115 U.S.A.

In the U.S.A. please add $1.50 for the first book or tape and
$.50 for each additional book or tape. Washington residents
add 8% sales tax.

Outside the U.S.A. please add $2.50 for the first book or tape
and $.60 for each additional book or tape.

Please send for our catalogue of books, audiotapes,
videotapes, and traditional spiritual literature.

INDEX

An Invitation

If you feel moved to consider Heart-Master Da Love-Ananda's Wisdom-Teaching further or to respond to his message of Happiness in any way, we of The Free Daist Communion open our doors and our hearts to assist you.

The Regional Centers of our Communion provide a variety of introductory presentations, programs, and courses that can accommodate many levels of interest.

For those who do not live near a Regional Center, there are study groups in cities throughout the world.

Additionally, the Regional Centers offer correspondence courses to assist your study of the Wisdom-Teaching of Da Love-Ananda in your own home.

For those who wish further involvement, the Friends Program will accommodate your interest through guided courses of study, instructive and sacred occasions at our Regional Centers around the world, and personal association with mature practitioners.

Over thirty volumes of the Teaching literature of Da Love-Ananda are available. Please write to the address below for a free catalogue of books, recorded audiotapes and videotapes of Heart-Master Da Love-Ananda, and selected traditional and contemporary spiritual literature. Or, send away for a free issue of *The Laughing Man* magazine.

If you would like more information about The Free Daist Communion or active forms of patronage and support, or if you would like to become a participating Friend, or if you would like to begin to practice the Way Taught by Da Love-Ananda, please write to this address:

The Laughing Man Institute
P.O. Box 12775
San Rafael, CA 94913-2775 U.S.A.

Or write or call any of the Regional Centers listed on pp. 139–41 in this volume.